OVER 150,000 C HWBI

SOFT SELL

THE NEW ART OF SELLING

TIM CONNOR, CSP
4th Edition

SOURCEBOOKS, INC.
NAPERVILLE, ILLINOIS

This publication is designed to provide accurate and authoritative in regard to the subject matter covered. It is sold with the understanding that the publisher is not engaged in rendering legal, accounting, or other professional service. If legal advice or other expert assistance is required, the services of a competent professional person should be sought.
—*From a Declaration of Principals Jointly Adopted by a committee of the American Bar Association and a Committee of Publishers and Associations.*

Published by Sourcebooks, Inc. P.O. Box 4410, Naperville, Illinois 60567-4410
(630) 961-3900   FAX: (630) 961-2168
www.sourcebooks.com

Library of Congress Cataloging-in-Publication Data

Connor, Tim
    Soft sell: the new art of selling, self empowerment,
and persuasion/Tim Connor. —4th ed.
        p.   cm.
    Includes index.
    ISBN 1-4022-0112-5 (alk. paper)
    1. Selling   2. Sales Management   I. Title
HF5438.25.C655   1998
658.85—dc21   98-7187
                                               CIP

Printed and bound in the United States of America
BG   10   9   8   7   6   5   4   3   2   1

In memory of all the great speakers and trainers who have passed on.

TABLE OF CONTENTS

FOREWORD

If this book is to have any lasting meaning for you as you travel life's journey, you must recognize one underlying fact: Life involves constant change—you must change and grow daily, weekly, yearly. If you refuse to grow, you will die—if not physically, then emotionally.

The purpose of this book is to help you change, help you grow and help you find peace, contentment, and success as you change.

The Thirteen Virtues

Ben Franklin at one time had an intolerable personality. He practiced the following 13 virtues and through them developed one of the outstanding personalities of all time. Memorize them, practice them and you also will have a personality worthy of emulation.

1. Temperance: Eat not to dullness. Drink not to elevation.
2. Silence: Speak not but what may benefit others or yourself. Avoid trifling conversation.
3. Order: Let all your things have their places. Let each part of your business have its time.

4. Resolution: Resolve to perform what you ought. Perform without fail what you resolve.

5. Frugality: Make not expense but to do good to others or yourself; i.e., waste nothing.

6. Industry: Lose no time. Be always employed in something useful. Cut off all unnecessary actions.

7. Sincerity: Use no hurtful deceit. Think innocently and justly; if you speak, speak accordingly.

8. Justice: Wrong none by doing injuries or omitting the benefits that are your duty.

9. Moderation: Avoid extremes. Forbear resenting injuries so much as you think they deserve.

10. Cleanliness: Tolerate no uncleanliness in body, clothes or habitation.

11. Tranquility: Be not disturbed at trifles or at accidents common or unavoidable.

12. Chastity: Rarely use venery but for health or offspring—never to dullness, weakness or the injury of your own or another's peace or reputation.

13. Humility: Imitate Jesus and Socrates. Let no pleasure tempt thee, no profit allure thee, no ambition corrupt thee, no example sway thee, no persuasion move thee, to do anything which thou knowest to be evil; so shalt thou always live jollily; for a good conscience is a continual Christmas.

SELLING AS AN OPPORTUNITY

Winning isn't everything, but wanting to win is.
—Vince Lombardi

I am the greatest. I said that even before I knew I was.
—Muhammad Ali

Education is a social process...
Education is growth...
Education is preparation for life; education is life itself.
—John Dewey

Life in the twentieth century is like a parachute jump; you have to get it right the first time.

—Margaret Mead

Introduction

Whether you've been selling for two days, two months, two years or a lifetime, or are thinking about entering the sales profession, you've had your ups and downs many times over. Commitment in every activity, especially professional selling, is one of the most important ingredients necessary if you are to succeed and be content in your success. The following may seem trite or corny to you but it is a necessary starting point. Take it at face value. What selling means to you and me may not be the same. But now, more than ever, we must face up, speak up, and tell the world our story if free enterprise and the competitive marketplace are to survive the rest of this century.

Selling is an opportunity. How did you happen to choose sales? Few people, I'm sure, ever played "salespeople games" as a child. At best, over the years the profession has been tarnished. And by and large, it is not due to a few bad apples, but by almost all of us and our "Let the rest of the profession take care of themselves" attitude. Are you proud of your position and role in the free marketplace? Did you know that the average professional salesperson keeps more than 30 people employed? This is a true opportunity to serve mankind.

Why is professional selling the third highest income group in our country? Certainly not because you failed at everything else and decided to "try sales" as a last resort, and certainly not because it's easy. It's a profession with the potential for high personal income and rewards in which you don't even need a high school diploma. That's opportunity! The success stories in selling come in all shades, sizes, ages, and colors. All you need to begin is a recognition of your opportunity to determine your own destiny, a commitment to yourself to succeed, and an almost inhuman capacity for work and failure. Don't expect everyone to either buy from or like you.

Selling is an obligation. If you've made your pledge to success in selling, then you must recognize your obligation to yourself, to your family, your customer, your company, and most of all, to your prospect.

You owe it to your prospect to improve his life or business if your product or service can provide the means. If it can't, you'd better change companies or redefine your prospects. To take your obligation seriously, you must believe in what you have to offer, then exchange it for your prospect's time and dollars. You have then, and only then, fulfilled your obligation to your prospect. He has the right to expect no less from a professional.

You owe it to yourself, for the health of your own self-image, to achieve success with your prospect. Tell me, do you feel as good at the end of five "nos" as you do at the end of five "yeses"? A positive self-image is vital to your success. Achievement provides a positive stimulus.

And you owe it to your company, because without it you don't have a product or service to sell.

So you see, you have an obligation to many people, institutions, and ideals. Selling, then, is an obligation. One that you cannot and should not take lightly if you are to successfully fulfill your role as a professional.

The price for success in selling is high but it's worth it, and usually the price for success is lower than the price for failure.

Selling is your right. In a free enterprise system, you have the right to fail and the right to succeed. You have the right to work the 10-, 14-, even 16-hour day. In selling you have the right to sell well into your 60s, 70s, and beyond. You have the right to determine your own future.

Why Sales Is a Great Profession

There is no other field of endeavor where an ambitious person can earn a larger income or pave the way to financial success with greater certainty and without working capital than in the field of selling. Age is no asset or liability. Mental attitude and character are.

I have trained salespeople to successful sales careers who started as young as 17 and as old as 65. Men and women, regardless of previous employment, have been motivated and trained to earn high incomes in their new vocations over a period of a few years. What's more important, they learned to love their work. Each expressed pride in the statement, "I am a salesperson." Each was motivated to realize the dignity, power, and prestige in becoming successful in a chosen sales career.

Sales Is a Great Profession Because:

1. You can determine what your future income will be and accomplish it.
2. You can combat inflation by working smarter.
3. Selling is fun. It's an enjoyable game when you become proficient.
4. You have personal security. You may in the future lose all of your tangible wealth. As a salesperson you can regain it if you are willing to start over again with the proper mental attitude.
5. You have unlimited opportunities for advancement along paths of your own choosing.
6. Because you know how to persuade others, you can influence your family and those closely associated with you to improve themselves.
7. You can render invaluable service to your community, your country, the competitive marketplace, and the free enterprise system.

You tell on yourself

You tell on yourself by the friends you seek,
 by the very manner in which you speak,
 by the way you employ your leisure time,
 by the use you make of dollars and time.
You tell what you are by the things you wear,
 by the spirit in which your burdens bear,
 by the kind of things at which you laugh,
 by the records you play on your phonograph.
You tell what you are by the way you walk,
 by the things of which you delight to talk,
 by the manner in which you bear defeat,
 by so simple a thing as how you eat.
By the books you choose from a well-filled shelf.
 in these ways and more, you tell on yourself.
 So there's really no particle of sense in an
 effort to keep up false pretense.
 You tell on yourself.

—Author unknown

Success Is Your Responsibility

*Some men see things as they are and say, "Why?" I dream things
that never were and say, "Why not?"*
—Robert F. Kennedy

We don't know each other, you and I, but through years of research and study of self-help literature and people in general, I think I know a little about you.

You are either casually or seriously committed to personal success. You have your own special brand of "What I want or what I think I want." I know, I've been there! Sometimes knowing and sometimes thinking I knew. I have felt the frustration, despair, and anxiety. If you are 100 percent committed to achieving what success means to you and ultimately are able to understand and consistently move in the direction of your personal goals, you will be in the top 5 percent of the people in the nation. Quite a distinction! But I know you, or most of you—you're like me. You want it and work for it, but there always seems to be some minor ingredient missing. You always seem to come so close, so very close.

The book you are holding is my attempt to share with you my trials, tribulations, successes, failures and why it took me more than 20 years and thousands of hours of study before these principles finally sank in. I hope to save you that time and some of that effort. Success involves choices which often mean sacrifices. You have a choice now! If you are not prepared to seriously work toward your life's dreams, add this book to your stack of texts that represent your feeble attempt at change. However, if you are fed up with frustration, anxieties, broken promises, and going without much of what you think you deserve, then commit today to change.

Habits die hard! What you are and what you do is the result of habit. You have created what you are today. If you are to change what you become you must form new habits. Either you will form new habits beginning today or your life will continue as in the past.

I don't have the answers to your life—you do! Somewhere in your mind of 15-20 billion brain cells is the potential for greatness. The choice to be great or leave your unlimited potential behind you is your decision.

Your future is up to you! Stop looking back. Look around you emotionally, psychologically, or physically; take the responsibility for where you are and where you go in life, and start today.

In the chapters that follow, I will, in simple terms and everyday language (I write the way I talk), present you with formulas, guidelines, methods, and ideas that can accelerate and facilitate your journey to personal sales success.

Warning

I don't know what your destiny will be, but one thing I know:
The only ones among you who will be really happy are those who
will have sought and found how to serve.

—Irving Berlin

However, only a small fraction of you will actually change—or even attempt to do anything permanent with the material covered. The interesting thing is that at this point—yes, right now—you know who you are.

This book has been written for you, not for the 5 percent. They don't need me or my ideas. Interestingly enough, however, the five percent will read it with more interest and commitment. They are constantly seeking even one new idea that will make them more productive. My personal goal is to share my years of study and their lessons with you in a way that will educate you, inspire you, but most of all, upset you. Yes, my goal as a salesperson, sales trainer, and author is to get under your skin, to be a thorn in your side, to make you feel very uncomfortable with yourself and your progress. If change is to take place on a consistent daily basis, the stimulus for that change must come from within you, not from me, your spouse, children, books, the environment, or any other outside force. If you skip any section, page, exercise, review question or problem, you are reaffirming your position in the 95 percent of the population of salespeople who never really find contentment, peace of mind, happiness, or any form of lasting success.

Tips on Using This Book to Aid Your Success

To get the most out of this self-help sales book, follow these suggestions: First, read a chapter completely, then go back, reread the chapter making notes and underlining key points. Next, go back a third time, answer the questions, do the exercises and problems and then translate your notes from the general to the specific. Ask yourself, "How can I use this idea selling my product or my service?"

Each honest calling, each walk of life, has it own elite, its own aristocracy based on excellence of performance.
—James B. Connant

Self-analysis Questionnaire

1. Why am I reading this book?
2. Am I satisfied with my professional progress? (Why or why not?)
3. Am I satisfied with my financial progress? (Why or why not?)
4. List of my personal assets and liabilities (not materialistic).

Assets

_____

_____

_____

Liabilities

_____

_____

_____

5. Have I been honest in appraising my assets and liabilities?
6. I believe my strongest assets are: (Why?)

_____

_____

_____

7. I believe my greatest weaknesses are: (Why?)

_____

_____

_____

8. Do I have the full support of my family as I move forward toward my goals? Why/why not?
9. Do I have the full support of my company manager, associates, etc.) as I move toward my goals? Why/why not?
10. Make a statement of your belief in yourself, your profession, and your product or service.
11. Do I have complete and up-to-date knowledge of my business?
12. Am I delivering better results day by day?

13. Are other people putting more pep into their work than I am into mine?
14. Do I get right down to business and think and plan as much as I should?
15. Am I as enthusiastic as I should be?
16. Am I giving as many hours as I should to my work each day? Each week?
17. Is there anything—personal business, pleasure, vices, debts or obligations—taking any part of my time or attention from my job and destroying my efficiency?
18. Am I giving the management my hearty support, or am I criticizing by word, deed, or thought?
19. Do I employ the company's methods or am I ignoring them?
20. Am I developing rapidly enough to keep in line with the company's progress?

How Am I Doing?

"Whatever the mind of man can conceive and believe, it can achieve."
—Napoleon Hill

In the turmoil of today, just where is the world headed? There is both temptation and excuse for any thoughtful person to wonder about that. If one listens only to the pessimists, he might yield to their obsession that the world is going to the devil fast. On the other hand, if one casts his lot with the Pollyannas, he is likely to be lulled to sleep dreaming contentedly of a world waxing wise and virtuous.

Neither view is normal. One drops us into a well of despair. The other exalts us on a pillar of pride. The former finds some foundation in the newspaper headlines day after day. The latter can be proved by a list of evils eliminated by civilization.

The world has not "gone to the dogs," neither has it reached the point where it does not need further improvement. If we want to see the world move toward a more perfect fellowship of man, the important thing is not to worry about the world, but to wonder about ourselves.

The big question is not "Is the world getting better?" but "Am I getting better?" Are the experiences I am having with life giving me a broader and more charitable outlook? Are my own disappointments teaching me empathy for others who are likewise disappointed? Are my own successes inspiring me to pause at the peak to offer a helping hand to someone still struggling up the hill? Can I look deep into my own heart and truthfully find that it is growing finer as it grows older?

If enough of us make up our minds to meet that test, the world will take care of itself.
—National Messenger

The Whole Salesperson

Attitude	People Skills	Selling Skills
belief	ask questions	prospecting
commitment	listening	sales presentations
desire	social styles	objections
ability to fail	psychological level	closing
persistent goals	body language	records
self-motivation	kinetics	service
enthusiasm		
purpose	**Product Knowledge**	
self-discipline	features	
confidence	uses	
creativity	applications	
empathy	product weaknesses	
go the extra mile	product strengths	
self-improvement	knowledge of the competition	
time organization		

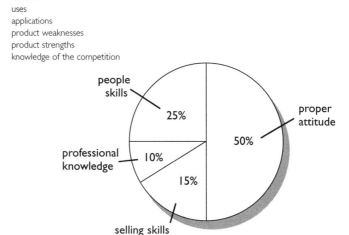

people
skills

25%

proper
attitude

50%

professional
knowledge

10%

15%

selling skills

The Salesman

And in those days, behold, there came through the gates of the city a sales-man from afar off, and it came to pass as the day went by he sold plenty.

And in that city were they that were the order-takers and they that spent their days in adding to the alibi sheets. Mightily were they astonished. They said one to the other, "What the hell; how doth he getteth away with it?" And it came to pass that many were gathered in the back office and a soothsayer came among them. And he was one wise guy. And they spoke and questioned him saying, "How is it that this stranger accomplished the impossible?"

Whereupon the soothsayer made answer: "He of whom you speak is one hustler. He ariseth very early in the morning and goeth forth full of pep. He complaineth not, neither doth he know despair. He is arrayed in purple and fine linen, while ye go forth with pants unpressed.

"While ye gather here and say one to the other, 'Verily this is a terrible day to work,' he is already abroad. And when the eleventh hour cometh, he needeth no alibis. He knoweth his line and they that would stave him off, they gave him orders. Men say unto him 'nay' when he cometh in, yet when he goeth forth he hath their names on the line that is dotted.

"He taketh with him the two angels 'inspiration' and 'perspiration' and worketh to beat hell. Verily I say unto you, go and do likewise."

—James X. Cahill

Millionaire Study

I recently completed a study of more than 50 millionaires. None of them started with any appreciable capital or inheritance. As a result of the study, a list of common traits emerged. The following is a list of those traits. Few of them actually had the goal to be a millionaire, but accumulated their wealth as a result of an idea, product or service. Many of those traits are also found in the most successful salespeople. They are not in any special order.

1. A legal mind or the ability to cut to the core of a problem or take charge of a situation quickly.
2. The habit of positive action
3. Hard work
4. Enthusiasm
5. A definite objective
6. Mentally tough
7. Physically fit
8. Became involved
9. Give more than they take
10. Learn to motivate
11. Loyalty
12. Learn from adversity
13. Strong commitment
14. Persistent
15. A risk-it-all attitude
16. Confidence

Suggested Reading

The following suggested reading list is offered as a self-improvement tool. As you complete reading each book, record the date.

Title	Date Started	Date Completed
The Bible		
Alesandra, Anthony, *Non-Manipulative Selling*		
Allen, James, *As a Man Thinketh*		
Anderson, U.S., *The Magic in Your Mind*		
Anderson, U.S., *Three Magic Words*		
Adizes, Ichak, *Corporate Lifecycles*		
Appleton, W., *Fathers and Daughters*		
Handler, Grinder, *Frogs Into Princes*		
Bach, *Bridge Across Forever, Illusions, Jonathan Livingston Seagull*		
Bencon, Herb, *The Mind Body Effect*		
Berg, Karen, *Get to the Point*		
Betger, Frank, *How I Raised Myself From Failure to Success in Selling*		
Blanchard, K., *One Minute Manager*		
Borg, Tom, *The Service Factor*		
Boyatzis, R., *The Competent Manager*		
Brande, Dorothea, *Wake Up and Live*		
Brandon, Nathanial, *Why Can't You Hear What I Can't Say*		
Bridges, William, *Transitions*		
Bristol, Claude M., *The Magic of Believing, The Power Within You*		
Brown, Barbara, *Superminds*		
Bry, Adeleide, *Directing the Movies of the Mind*		
Burns, Walter, *How Six Selling Steps Jumped My Income from $85-$1100 a Week*		
Butterworth, Eric, *Discover the Power Within You*		
Carnegie, Dale, *How To Win Friends and Influence People*		

Title	Date Started	Date Completed
Cetron, Marvin, *American Renaissance*		
Chopra, Deepak, *Unconditional Life, Ageless Body Timeless Mind*		
Clauson, George, *The Richest Man in Babylon*		
Clavell, James, *The Art of War*		
Connor, Tim, *Soft Sell*		
Conwell, Russell, *Acres of Diamonds*		
Cook, W., Success, *Motivation, and the Scriptures*		
Cooper, Frank, *The Customer Signs Your Paycheck*		
Copeland. K., *The Laws of Prosperity*		
Corbin, Carolyn, *Strategies 2000*		
Cousins, N., *Human Options*		
Deal, Terrance, *Corporate Cultures*		
Depree, Max, *Leadership is an Art*		
DeVos, Rich., *Believe*		
Dobson, J., *Emotions—Can You Trust Them?, What Wives Wish Their Husbands Knew About Women*		
Dossley, Larry, *Space, Time and Medicine*		
Downing, C., *The Cinderella Complex*		
Drucker, Peter, *The Effective Executive*		
Dunn, David, *Try Giving Yourself Away*		
Dyer, Wayne, *Erroneous Zones, The Sky's the Limit, Pulling Your Own Strings, You'll See It When You Believe It*		
Exton, William, *Motivation Leverage, Sales Leverage*		
Feldman, Ben, *Autobiography*		
Frankel, Victor, *Man's Search for Meaning*		
Frederick C., *Playing the Game the New Way*		
Gardner, John, *Self Renewal*		
Gibran, Kahlil, *The Prophet*		
Gifford, F., *Gifford on Courage*		
Gillies, J., *Money Love*		
Glasser, William, *The Identity Society, Control Theory*		

Title	Date Started	Date Completed
Goldratt, Eliyahu, *The Goal*		
Haldane, Bernard, *How To Make a Habit of Success*		
Harman, Bill, *Global Mind Change*		
Hill, Napoleon, *Think and Grow Rich Through Persuasion, Laws of Success, Think and Grow Rich*		
Hooper, D., *You Are What You Think*		
James, Muriel/Jongeward, Dorothy, *Born To Win*		
Johnson, Kerry, *Peak Performance Selling*		
Jones, Charles T., *Life is Tremendous*		
Keyes, Ken, *Your Life Is a Gift*		
Koren/Goodman, *The Haglers Handbook*		
Korda, Michael, *Power, Success*		
Kurtz, Sheila, *Graphotypes*		
Laidlaw, R., *The Reason Why*		
Lakein, Alan, *How to Get Control of Your Time and Your Life*		
Lazarus, Arnold, *In the Mind's Eye*		
Leider, Richard, *The Power of Purpose*		
Lewis, C.S., *Miracles, The Problem of Pain*		
Lucas & Lorayne, *The Memory Book*		
MacKenzie, R. Alec, *The Time Trap*		
Maltz, Maxwell, *Creative Living for Today, Psycho-Cybernetics*		
Mandino, Og, *The Greatest Salesman in the World, The Greatest Secret in the World, The Greatest Miracle in the World, The Christ Commission, University of Success*		
Marston, John, *The Emotions of Normal People*		
Maslow, Abraham, *Motivation and Personality*		
McLelland, Dave, *The Achieving Society*		
McWilliams, Peter/John-Roger, *Life 101, Wealth 101*		

Title	Date Started	Date Completed
Meninger, Karl, *Success Through Transactional Analysis*		
Miccali, Paul J., *Shortcuts to Impressive Speaking —How to Put Yourself Across, The Lacy Techniques of Salesmanship*		
Miller, A., *Prisoners of Childhood*		
Miller, Robert, *Conceptual Selling*		
Millman, Dan, *The Way of the Peaceful Warrior, The Sacred Journey of the Peaceful Warrior*		
Molloy, John T., *Dress for Success*		
Mortell, Arthur, *Anatomy of a Successful Salesman*		
Nierenburg, Gerald, *How to Read A Person Like a Book*		
Patent, Arnold, *You Can Have It All*		
Peale, Norman Vincent, *Enthusiasm Makes The Difference, The Positive Principle Today, The Power of Positive Thinking*		
Peck, Scot, *The Road Less Travelled*		
Powell, John, *Unconditional Love, Fully Human, Fully Alive*		
Prather, H., *Notes to Myself*		
Robbins, Tony, *Personal Power*		
Robert, Cavett, *Human Engineering & Motivation*		
Roberts, Wes, *Leadership Secrets of Attila the Hun*		
Rogers, Carl, *On Becoming A Person*		
Rogers, W., *Letters of a Self-Made Diplomat to His President*		
Rutherford, Bob, *Time Power*		
Schuller, Robert, *You Can Be The Person You Want To Be, Self love: The Dynamic Force of Success, Daily Power Thoughts*		
Sharpe, Robert, *The Success Factor*		
Sinetar, Marsha, *Do What You Love and the Money Will Follow*		
Stiller, Richard, *Habits*		

Title	Date Started	Date Completed
Stone, W. Clement, *The Success System That Never Fails*		
Sugarman, Joseph, *Success Forces*		
Symington/Creighton, *Getting Well Again*		
Tiger, Lionel, *Optimism, The Biology of Hope*		
Toffler, Alvin, *Future Shock, The Third Wave*		
Tozer, A.W., *The Pursuit of God*		
Trisler, Hank, *No Bull Selling*		
Waitly, Dennis, *The Psychology of Winning*		
Ziglar, Zig, *See You At The Top*		
Zukav, Gary, *Seat of the Soul*		

The Ten Selling Rules

These ten selling rules are the fundamentals of selling. In the simplest terms, the basics.

1. Your ability to control and direct the thinking of your prospect is directly related to your ability to control and direct your own thinking.

2. Your prospect's enthusiasm for your product or service is a product of your enthusiasm for your product or service.

3. Your ultimate success in sales depends on your ability to consistently maintain a high "new prospect awareness."

4. If you can only master one skill in selling, become a master prospector. It will guarantee your future success.

5. Judge your ability to give a good sales presentation by your ability to listen. You'll sell more by listening than talking.

6. Determine what your prospects want and desire, not what they need. Needs are logical; wants and desires are emotional.

7. Closing a sale requires only one attitude—the will to win. Only one skill—the ability to visualize your prospect as buying before you close.

8. Sales objections are as important to a successful sale as having a product or service to sell. Welcome them, encourage them, and answer them.

9. Sales records are an absolute must—keep them, analyze them, learn from them.
10. There is one attitude that separates winners from losers in sales—a service attitude. Your customer expects it, and deserves it. If he doesn't get it, he'll do business with your competitor.

When the game's over, it's really just beginning.
—Jerry Kramer

Sales Strategies of Six-Figure-Income Salespeople

It is unfortunate today that many salespeople are still following the "old standard" of planning their calls on their clients and prospects.

Rather than rehash these trite and outdated approaches, I would like to share the philosophies and attitudes with you that are being used by the successful salespeople of today and will be used by the superstars of tomorrow.

One. Who are you? What are your opinions, prejudices, judgments, attitudes, values, beliefs, philosophies, and old baggage that may be sabotaging your sales success. Do you know who you really are? Do you know who you take into your sales calls? Are you sending a non-verbal message that is consistent with your verbal behavior? How would your prospects and clients describe your behavior and attitudes?

A thorough, honed self-appraisal and subsequent modification of incorrect attitudes and behavior is critical for autonomy and success in selling in the new business climate.

Two. What is your basic fundamental purpose and mission in selling? Is it to make money? Serve your clients? Grow your company? Contribute to society? Provide for your family's current and future needs? Have fun? Enjoy the opportunity to determine your own career and financial destiny? What aspect of selling do you really feel passionate about? Would you change careers for more praise, recognition, challenge, responsibility, money, or opportunity?

Your reasons, more than your goals for staying in this demanding, challenging, and rewarding career will determine your peace, balance, and fulfillment as you walk the highway into your future sales career.

Three. What type of people do you like to be around? How do you like to spend your career time? What else is important to you in your life besides your career? How do you like to spend your personal time? What are your needs for career and personal stimulation and feelings of worth-whileness? Are they being satisfied in your current selling position or circumstances?

Selling today is about building successful, positive, on-going relationships—all types of relationships. Your overall success will be greatly impacted by your willingness and ability to establish and maintain positive relationships with everyone who is directly and indirectly connected with your sales success.

Four. How much time are you devoting to your personal and spiritual growth? Do you regularly read good books, listen to great audio tapes, attend seminars, and network with people who can help you? Do you take time to recharge your battery with vacations or weekend adventures? Do you take time to relax? Do you get adequate rest and proper nutrition?

A successful selling career requires lots of stamina, energy, and passion. You can't have these if you abuse your mind and body.

Five. Solving your prospects' or clients' problems is no longer an effective sales strategy. The successful salespeople in today's marketplace and the marketplace of tomorrow will be creative problem creators. Effective salespeople will be ruthless in their pursuit to uncover or create an awareness of problems clients weren't even aware they had. They will think far ahead of their clients, not just along with them.

If you want to guarantee your success in the coming years, you need only one approach. Find out what is preventing your prospects from getting a good night's sleep. Determine what is keeping them up at night worrying and you won't have to worry about customer loyalty, reducing prices, or over-aggressive competition.

Even poor salespeople can solve a client's problem with the right product, service, feature, or approach. It will take creative, forward-looking, and imaginative thinking to excel as the next millennium approaches.

Six. People buy from people they trust, not people they like. The key to building trust is simple. Promise a lot, and deliver more. Do what you say you will do and then some. Honor your commitments, communicate with integrity, and be a resource for your client, not just a salesperson selling a product or service.

I am a trainer, a speaker, and a consultant, but I don't actively sell myself as any of these. I do, however, sell myself as a client resource. What can you offer your client other than your products or services? You can provide a continuous flow of ideas. You can be an idea gold mine. But in order to be able to provide this level of information, you must first take a great deal of new information into your consciousness with regularity. Information is always available about the marketplace, your clients' businesses, human behavior, and a wide variety of current events that impact your business and the business of your clients and prospects.

I am not talking here about devouring the local newspaper or evening news. Constant reminders of what is wrong in the world or your hometown are not going to help you one bit in your selling or your ability to maintain a positive attitude or consciousness. I am referring here to subscribing to publications that feed your mind positive and worthwhile information—publications that help you keep in touch with how you can improve your selling behavior or the changing circumstances or trends in your target or niche industries.

Peak performance salespeople study their clients' business, their industry, their competition, and are walking encyclopedias of information on their own products and services. Anything less, and you are fair game for anyone and everyone to take your business away from you.

Seven. Successful salespeople don't sell price. They sell value. The price will always seem high if value is perceived as low. When you focus on price either because of poor product knowledge, poor client knowledge, or poor sales skills, you will always lose in the long run. Clients don't want cheap; they want the best value for their dollar. If you are focusing on price, you will never make it big in this dynamic profession. However, if you always sell value, you will never have to worry about losing business to price competition. Oh yes, in the short-term, you might lose a sale here or there. But if you are in this business for the long haul for both your company and your client, sooner or later your prospects or clients will come back to you and the value they need and desire.

Poor salespeople believe that prospects buy for price alone or as their major motivator. I won't try to convince you otherwise; I'll let you learn this one in the marketplace.

Eight. Effective prospecting is the most important sales skill you will ever need to master. It is more important than good closing techniques, good sales presentations, or the ability to answer client resistance. The best salespeople are at their best when they are getting information. If I have heard it once, I have heard it a million times—plan your sales presentation. Bull. When you plan your sales presentation, you are making a basic assumption that everyone who buys from you is going to buy for the same reason. If you have been selling for more than thirty days, you know this just isn't true. I can remember in my first sales position in the insurance industry over twenty-five years ago that I was told to memorize my presentation, my answers to objections, and my closes. Then I was to go out and deliver the company story. I was fired in six months because I found out that no one was interested in my company's story. The prospects wanted me to learn their stories. The job of professional selling is to discover prospect/client wants, needs, desires, opinions, problems, prejudices, attitudes, and/or judgments.

The most important element of the sales process for successful salespeople is not the giving of information but the getting of information. They don't plan their sales presentations but have a presentation strategy. If you have been selling your product or service for over three months, you should know what to say and when without planning it.

The pros never go into a sales situation, however, without planning their questions and the information they are going to get. Remember, your prospect will tell you what you need to tell them to sell them.

But you have to ask. And please don't forget, the information you don't get will cost you sales or sales relationships later.

Nine. An effective sales presentation is not a presentation but a conversation. A two-way conversation, not a one-way conversation. Many salespeople have been trained to deliver their sales message. This message is often a programmed discussion of the various features and benefits of their product or service. This approach to selling has never been used by the real pros. It is not an effective way to represent the product or service in the most professional manner, and it is certainly not in the best interests of the prospect or the goal of making a new client relationship. Successful salespeople are more concerned about getting a client than making a sale.

Every prospect buys for their reasons, not those of the salesperson or the company. When you deliver your standard approach or presentation, you are assuming that each prospect buys for the same reasons, at the same time, and in the same way. This just isn't true. Nor does it make good sense to sell this way. The successful salesperson customizes each sales conversation to the buying style, needs, interests, desires, and problems of each buyer. They don't try to shove their buying reasons or features down the throat of the customer.

Ten. Sales resistance from the client or prospect gives you valuable insight into their thinking. Successful salespeople don't try to maneuver around this resistance but get it into the open as soon as possible. Price is a good example. A confident salesperson who knows the value of their products and services doesn't run and hide from price objections. They bring up early in the sales process the value of working with a quality supplier. They are not afraid of their product or service inadequacies. They know that the other aspects of their organization, personal service, or value-added approach more than makes up for what they don't have or can't provide. No product or service is ever perfect for every prospect in every potential situation. Sooner or later, every prospect must go without something. The approach of successful salespeople is to insure that the prospect understands that what they are getting more than makes up for what they are missing, and also understands how the product or service will satisfy their needs, desires, problems, or opportunities.

The myth is that you should be able to sell everyone sooner or later. I wish this were true. It would make selling so much easier. But the reality is that not everyone in the marketplace is a good prospect for you, now or in the future. They may be a prospect, but not the best one for the time, energy and resources you have available at the present time. Timing is critical in successful selling. But given the tremendous amount of potential new business in the world today, I believe it is suicide to take the time, energy, and corporate resources to try and turn poor prospects into customers or clients. As an aside, if you are able to sell a poor prospect for whatever reason, you will often find they cause you the most stress and are generally not worth it. Some companies have a strategy that in order to sell successfully in a particular market or to a certain prospect, you must take business that is not profitable, does not fit your customer mix, or does not help you attain your long-term objectives. I have never subscribed to this philosophy.

The key to successful selling is your ability to always be in front of the most qualified prospects or clients, not just any prospects or clients.

Eleven. Closing the sale is not a matter of trick closes or manipulation. It is not using fear, guilt, or hard-sell tactics. Closing the sale on a well-qualified prospect is the natural conclusion to everything you have done in the sales process that is correct and effective. You can make people buy things they don't need, but you can't make people buy things they don't want. Poor salespeople try to turn poor prospects into customers or clients. Good salespeople identify good prospects early in the process and help them get what they want. They accomplish this with good listening skills, a lot of client or prospect understanding, and a willingness to be flexible and compromise.

The key to successful closing is effective prospecting.

Twelve. After sales, service is the glue that keeps clients loyal, buying more, and willing to give you referrals and positive references. The best salespeople work as hard to keep their clients as they did to get them. They understand that clients will always have new choices for the services or products that they sell. To keep their clients satisfied, they constantly conduct client reality checks. They are always checking client perceptions and attitudes. Poor salespeople take the money and run.

One lesson that the best salespeople have learned is that it is always easier and less costly to do more business with a present client than it is to keep finding new clients. They put just as much of their time, energy, and resources into keeping clients and building client relationships as they do looking for new clients.

I am sure if you have been selling for a number of years, you have probably taken issue with some of my points in this chapter. That's good. I hope I have triggered some thinking on your part. Old school salespeople, those that are unwilling to adapt or change their approaches or strategies, are stuck in outdated perceptions and realities.

All I ask you to do is reexamine your selling philosophies in light of current market and consumer trends. I am confident that some of you need to refocus some of your attitudes and approaches if you are going to excel in the sales profession in the years ahead.

CONTROLLING YOUR ATTITUDES

SELLING RULES: NUMBER 1 & 2

1. Your ability to control and direct the thinking of your prospect is directly related to your ability to control and direct your own thinking.

2. Your prospect's enthusiasm for your product or service is a product of your enthusiasm for your product or service.

Chapter Objectives

1. To help you better know yourself and know how your thinking affects the sales process.

2. To turn the responsibility for your success over to you and away from your environment.

3. To master the techniques necessary for dealing with fear, failure, and rejection.

4. To help you better understand the concepts of success and motivation.

2

Observe all men, thyself most.

—Ben Franklin

Would you live with ease, do what you ought, and not what you please. Success has ruined many a man.

—Ben Franklin

Introduction

You and I have one thing in common—we have arrived psychologically and mentally at our current status through a similar route. We may have been brought up by different parents in different parts of the country, we may not be the same sex, religion, color, age, or nationality, but believe me, we have one major trait in common—we have both been conditioned by an environment over which we had no control. Our early childhood (for most of us prior to age 7) has more to do with our current level of success than any other single factor.

Search others for their virtues, thyself for thy vices.

—Ben Franklin

Early Conditioning

Most psychologists agree that by age 7 or 8 we have decided what kind of a person we are, what we will become, how our world will respond or react to us, what kind of people we are going to deal with, and what our environment will be. Most of us could not choose our parents, our date of birth, color, sex, or place of birth. These physical and geographical characteristics were already in place when we began our life. We weren't born positive or negative, self-disciplined, enthusiastic or unenthusiastic salespeople, lawyers, or doctors. We all came into this world the same—naked babies with neither good nor bad habits. Through our exposure to our environment, our parents, grandparents, teachers, friends, and society, we developed certain mental pictures of ourselves. We formed mental habits of thinking and physical habits of action. In a sense we could not choose our circumstances, but these circumstances now exert a great deal of influence on us and our daily conscious activities.

Recent experiments with various laboratory animals clearly show how a conditioning environment can control an animal's behavior forever, or until a new set of conditioned habits are established. For example, in an aquarium in Canada, scientists placed pike in the same tank with a school of minnows, and separated them by a glass partition. After repeatedly crashing into the glass barrier, the pike finally resigned himself to circling around in the tank, happy to remain hungry, watching the minnows on the other side. Then the glass partition was removed. Guess what? You're right, the pike still remained on his side of the "imagined barrier." (See Figure 2-A.)

Figure 2-A

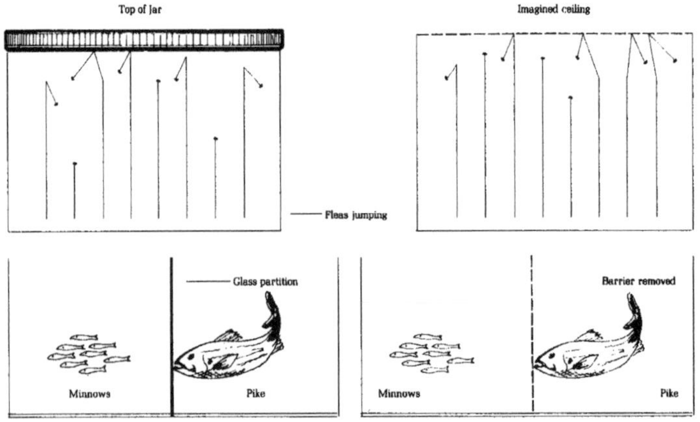

Have you ever been to a circus and seen a full-grown bull elephant circling a wooden stake with a thin rope? Ever wonder why he just doesn't pull out the stake, break the rope, and roam free through the circus grounds? He can't, and the reason is simple. As a baby elephant, he was conditioned not to wander by having a thick stainless steel stake hammered several feet into the ground, with a heavy steel chain from the stake to his ankle. He won't even try to move. Why? His present actions are controlled by his previous conditioning.

Put fleas in a jar and watch them as they bounce off the inside of the top. You'll notice after a time that the fleas will continue to jump, but short of the top! They have conditioned themselves to jump just so high. Then, take the top off! They could jump out now, but they don't. Their current actions are based on the earlier conditioning experiences.

Unfortunately, you and I are just like the pike, the flea, and the elephant. We have been told or have come to believe certain things about life and ourselves that are either not true, half-true or negative. Many of our current conscious actions are based on early exposures and conditioning.

Transactional Analysis Approach to Conditioning

Another, more scientific, way to look at this is to look at some of the research our transactional analysis psychologist friends have done. They developed the tape recorder theory. According to this theory, the day you were born three tape recorders turned on in your head. These tape recorders have been labeled ego states: the parent ego state, the adult ego state, and the child ego state. These recorders have recorded everything that's ever happened to you along with the emotion you felt as the experience was actually taking place. Both the experience and the emotion were then permanently stored in the subconscious for immediate recall whenever necessary. The problem is that much of what was appropriate self-learned or taught behavior as a child is not necessarily appropriate as an adult. In addition, a lot of information we have stored is either not true or not in our best interest as we mature. (See Figure 2-B)

The parent ego state recorded all the do's and don'ts, should's and should not's, and rules of living. Let me illustrate. Please complete the following sentences: Children should be seen and not_____. Don't bite off more than you can_____. Don't go where you're not_____. Don't speak unless you're _____. Don't ever speak to_____. How did you do? Try this experiment on an associate or friend. You will be amazed. The answers will be the same and yet even though you and your friend haven't heard these statements for years, you'll never forget them. They have been ingrained into your subconscious.

Yet, to be successful in sales, you have to do all of these things. Would you be interested to know the major cause of failure in sales? It's the fear of rejection. Now, where do you think that fear originates? Reread the past several sentences, and you'll have the answer.

The subconscious conditioned reflex is in control of your conscious activity. You want to call on people. You and I are in the people business. We don't sell products or services. We sell ideas and solutions to people, and people sell our products and services to themselves. The only way to eliminate the fear of rejection is to record a new set of internal tapes which causes a new behavior pattern that replaces the playing or the original fear-of-rejection tape that was made early in life. You can't erase these old tapes, but you can create new ones and thus turn off the old inappropriate reactions. This is the role of the adult tape recorder—to take learned parent information and update it with reality. Let me give you an example.

Many people overlearn from experience. Mark Twain tells a story about a cat that sat on a hot stove. That cat never sat on another hot stove again. He never sat on a cold one either. He just got out of the business of sitting on stoves. He overlearned from experience.

Our adult ego state is responsible for updating archaic parent data, making it possible to live in reality, and function in a mature world.

The child ego state recorded all the emotion—love, fear, hate, joy, excitement. Most people would like to act like a child if they thought they could get away with it. But we are all concerned with what other people think. We don't want to make fools of ourselves, unless, of course, we've had too much to drink at a party or are cheering the hometown team. Many or us are living in our childhood psychologically with one exception—we're not children. "Don't do this! Don't do that! Why do you ask so many questions? Here, let Mommy and Daddy help you." And the list goes on. "You can't do this! You don't have the looks, money, education,

Figure 2-B
THE ROLE OF EACH EGO STATE

PARENT
EGO
STATE
- Do's and Don'ts
- Should's and Should not's
- Rules of living
- Prejudice

ADULT
EGO
STATE

Blends what was taught as a child with reality to function more productively in the present.

CHILD
EGO
STATE

Emotions: love, joy, fear, wants, excitement

THE MIND

Self-Image

Conscious mind knows the difference between real and imaginary

Subconscious mind cannot determine between what is real and that which we vividly imagine

The mind is an iceberg—it floats with one one-seventh of its bulk above water.

—Sigmund Freud

experience. No one in our family has ever done that. You can't do that, you're too old, too young. You're black, a woman..." Enough—this scenario is repeated a million times a day and inhibits personal growth.

You have an internal dialogue between the conscious and subconscious that goes on night and day at the rate of several hundred words a minute. What kinds of things are we saying to ourselves? "I can't remember names. Everything I eat turns to fat. I am what I am, I can't change. I'm not good-looking. I can't do anything right. I'm clumsy. I can't get ahead." The list of self-defeating dialogue is endless.

The ego states of people are intricately involved in the purchase of products, buying decisions and emotions.

- The **child** wants a new car, home, computer, suit, copy machine, club membership, etc.
- The **adult** makes the decision to buy or not to buy.
- The **parent** okays the decision of the adult.

Exercise

For the next 48 hours listen to your own internal dialogue or self-talk. That dialogue is reinforcing your early beliefs and decisions in life. Before you can change, you must become aware of this inner dialogue. (See Figure 2-C)

Figure 2-C
INTERNAL DIALOGUE RECORDER

WHAT I AM SAYING	WHAT IT MEANS

Now that we've discussed what happens, let's talk about how it happens. Complete another sentence if you will. "Pepsi Cola hits the_____." Yes; "spot." But you haven't heard that since 1954—nearly 40 years ago. Pepsi stopped using that promotion in its advertising, but you will never forget it. Why? Because Pepsi drilled that into our heads (or sub-conscious) using one simple learning concept—repetition. All good advertising uses repetition. "I'd walk a mile for a_____." "Coca Cola, the pause that_____." "Winston tastes good_____." Our parents and environment have used this same teacher very effectively; consider the little child who wants to speak to strangers, but whose parents have told him or her repeatedly not to. Try a little experiment the next time you are walking around a shopping center. Say "hello" to ten adults and ten children (all strangers) and watch the various reactions.

Conditioning and Success

How does all this conditioning affect our productivity? You and I have a self-image. All that we are or do must pass through this self-image. Think of it as a grid. When it is more negative, the grid is tighter and restricts growth, creativity, and accomplishment. When it is more positive, it is wider and the opposite benefits are possible. We have a self-image in all our roles and activities in life.

Now, let's relate this to the sales profession. Most people in sales have a self-imposed ceiling of thinking. (See Figure 2-D) This ceiling is not a physical barrier, but an internal mental one. It's almost like an internal quota. Most salespeople who have ever worked under a quota system will agree that the average salesperson quits when he reaches his quota. The same is true when we reach our internal quota or self-imposed ceiling. Let's say that your average month's sales are $100,000. Next month, in the first three weeks, you reach $80,000. What will you generally do the fourth week? The following month, let's say you reach the $80,000 in the first week. Generally, we will reach our additional $20,000, hitting our ceiling, over the three-week period. In working with salespeople and companies as a trainer for more than 15 years, I have found that this internal quota rule governs most salespeople and therefore most sales organizations. This self-imposed ceiling effectively limits how we perform.

Figure 2-D
THE SUBCONSCIOUS

DO YOU KNOW WHERE YOUR IMAGINARY CEILING IS?

How can you change your imaginary ceiling? Before an idea can become a part of our automatic daily conscious activity, that idea must be firmly embedded into our subconscious mind. The information must pass through the conscious state. In other words, you must read the book several times—listen to the cassette several times—attend the seminar several times—before the subconscious mind finally accepts the idea. When it does, it will affect conscious activity.

How to Eliminate Your Self-imposed Ceiling of Thinking

Generally accepted theories in self-help psychology today contend that people can modify behavior to change their outcomes in life. Some people require a significant emotional event such as divorce, a heart attack, or business failure before they realize the need for change in their thought patterns or performance.

The good news is that we needn't wait for disaster to strike before we begin the development of new, more positive habits. To raise one's self-imposed limitations or to begin to see life or ourselves as limitless requires only a change in outlook, belief, interpretation, or perception. We need only to change our mind. This is an easy decision to make but a difficult one for many to carry out with commitment and consistency.

I believe one of the premises in Peter and John-Roger McWilliams's book, Life 101—that you can have anything you want, but you can't have everything you want.

The procedure is simple: Decide what it is you want. Dedicate yourself to its achievement, focus all of your thoughts, actions and energy to its attainment and be ruthless in your pursuit. Move around, through, above, or under your obstacles. Move steadily and patiently forward with a singleness of purpose and passion and you will be astonished at how your limitations melt away. Previous setbacks, discouragement, problems or failures will become insignificant. You will experience new levels of performance, satisfaction, success, and happiness. Limitations are all self-imposed. All discovery is self-discovery.

The Subconscious

There is one very profound and interesting fact surrounding the conscious and subconscious mind. The conscious mind can distinguish between what is real and what is imaginary—but the subconscious cannot. The subconscious does not know the difference between a real experience and one that has been vividly imagined. It does not know the difference between a real failure and one that is imagined. Likewise, it does not know the difference between a real success and an imagined success. The subconscious mind also resists a new idea the first time it is exposed to it.

This is one of the vital keys to success. Please reread this paragraph. Believe it or not—it is one of the most powerful statements you will ever read. You can literally persuade your subconscious mind through the use of repetition into believing something is true even when it is not. When it believes, it will cause subconscious activity to create the conditions it believes are already true. Think about this a minute.

What this means is that if we control our thoughts, we can control our circumstances and conditions. And we can control our thoughts if we choose to do so. Where can you make the perfect sales call—the one where you say everything just right and do everything just right, and the prospect also does and says everything just as you would like him to? In your mind. If you will practice repeatedly the perfect sales call in your own mind, imagine how powerful the belief of your subconscious mind will be as it relates to your conscious ability to give only perfect sales calls.

WHAT THE MIND ATTENDS TO, THE MIND CONSIDERS.
WHAT THE MIND DOES NOT CONSIDER, THE MIND DISMISSES.
WHAT THE MIND CONTINUALLY CONSIDERS, THE MIND BELIEVES.
WHAT THE MIND BELIEVES, THE MIND EVENTUALLY DOES.

You and I move toward the thoughts that dominate our minds. We literally become what we think about. Plato said: "Take charge of your thoughts and you can do what you will with them." The Bible says: "Whatsoever a man thinketh in his heart, so is he."

Recent research into psychosomatic medicine reveals that much of our physical and mental ailments and diseases (up to 75-80 percent) are caused by our own thinking or emotions. Are you aware of what causes ulcers? Worry and stress, and both of these ailments are in the mind. If we get sick in the mind, can we get well in the mind? Dr. Symington, in his excellent book *Getting Well Again*, is curing terminally ill cancer patients in his clinic in Texas by teaching people to repeatedly visualize the cancer cells dying and being flushed from the body. One key factor in his system, if it is to be successful, is a strong belief on the part of the patient that the method is working.

Dr. Lionel Tiger, in his book *Optimism, the Biology of Hope*, suggests that optimistic people live healthier and longer lives than pessimistic people.

This book is not a treatise on biology, but in my personal experience, one thing is very clear. When I knew and believed positively that I was going to make a sale, I usually did; and when there was any doubt, I seldom closed the sale. In closing this section let me suggest that if you can't convince yourself that your prospect is going to buy, I seriously doubt that you'll ever be able to convince him. The most important sale is to yourself. Again, where can you make the perfect sales presentation every time? In your mind. If you practice making perfect sales presentations in your mind with belief and repetition, you will eventually improve your actual presentations.

It is often easier to fight for one's principles than to live up to them.
—Adlai Stevenson

Figure 2-E

LEARNING THROUGH REPETITION

New Habit Practice
To move a habit from conscious
will to subconscious belief
requires constant repetition until
the subconscious believes the
habit has been formed.

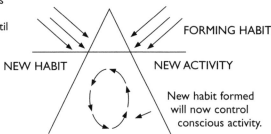

FORMING HABIT

NEW HABIT   NEW ACTIVITY

New habit formed
will now control
conscious activity.

Success as a Concept

My objective is not to tell you what you have to do to become successful, nor is it to tell you what I did to become successful. Rather, it is to share a few general ideas with you on what many people through the years have developed on this intriguing concept—success!

As a point of reference, I believe that if we break down this concept into its smallest parts, the whole idea becomes clearer and more exciting.

You've heard it said that success is a journey, not a destination, and that success must involve goals. But here is where many of the success prophets (or profits, depending on your perspective) leave us hanging. If success is a journey, where did it begin and where, if ever, does it end? (See Figure 2-F)

Are we destined to never arrive somewhere? How do we know whether we're still traveling ahead or whether we're merely like the squirrel on the rotating cylinder? Most people run like crazy forever and never seem to get anywhere.

Success is first a personal thing. It is different things to different people. What are you after? What's important to you? You! Not your spouse, sales manager or your children. You must first recognize that you are different from others. Your wants are different, your needs are different, your problems are different, your life is different; therefore, your goals must be different.

Figure 2-F
WHERE ARE YOU SUCCESSFUL

SUCCESS JOURNEY

Success must involve goals. Man is a striving, goal-seeking, growing organism. If we are not growing, we are dying. Abraham Maslow, in his excellent book, *Motivation and Personality*, states that "no matter how old you are, the day you can't sit down and come up with a want list, you're in trouble, you're on your way out." Statistics over the years have shown that the average person that retires at age sixty-five lives an average of four to seven years. The reason has become clear. Their goal all their lives was to retire. The goal was reached. Now they sit with no new goals and slowly die.

These goals must be worthwhile—worthwhile to you. You'll never be able to get excited about someone else's goals unless they are related to your own. The goals must stretch you ever so slightly, and they must have value for you. They must also be progressive. The important thing to remember is that it's not what you get when you achieve your goal that's important, but what you have become in the process.

Defining Success

We have just defined success. It is the progressive realization of a worth-while, predetermined, personal goal. You are not successful the day you achieve your goal, but rather on the day you set the direction and keep moving. I have a sign over my desk that summarizes this concept: "You Never Fail Until You Stop Trying."

Unfortunately, the vast majority of people look at success as a comparison—"I'm doing better than my father, brother, neighbor, associates, last year"—this becomes an easy cop-out for many. If your success has only to do with who or what you compare yourself with in your environment, then you will always be successful. Only a fool would compare himself with someone who is better off, smarter, luckier, better-looking. This idea of comparison to determine your success is ludicrous, but why do many people fall into this obvious trap? It begins early in childhood. Little Johnny comes home from school, complaining that Bobby has more toys, a nicer house, a bigger dad, more freedom, more, more, more. His success is not what he is or has, but what he is or has in relation to his environment.

Then, Johnny goes to school for several years and two or three times a year he comes home with a report card of grades. Those grades are not an indication of how smart Johnny is, but how smart he is compared to his classmates, some artificial norm, or a teacher's opinion of his ability. Again, Johnny's success is not what he is or has, but what he is or has compared to his environment. Johnny now goes into the world and begins this rat race to keep up with, yes, the "Joneses." He buys autos, homes, clothes, takes vacations, joins clubs, and more to show the world, "Look! I'm successful."

Johnny goes into sales in a company with thirty salespeople and his goal is to be #1. But there can be only one #1. Does that mean that every-one else is a failure? Your success is not a comparison of you to me, your environment or your past. If you must compare, your success is a compar-ison of you to your potential. You do not have the right to judge me based on your definition of success and neither do I have the right to judge you.

I recently gave a speech before one hundred very successful business executives. I seldom wear a suit. Picture, if you will, my being intro-duced to this sophisticated group of business owners and my subject is success. You could see it in their faces, "This kid is going to talk to us about success? He doesn't look old enough, smart enough. He doesn't even dress the part!" They were judging—and many of them missed my message because they let their own definition of success get in the way of some new and potentially valuable information. You and I live in a very role-oriented, judgmental society. We judge people on their roles or external conditions. This can be dangerous and misleading.

'Tis easier to prevent bad habits than to break them.
—Ben Franklin

Success and Your Habits

Where are you right now? Where would you like to be right now? Yes, today. Do you know why you're not there? I have one observation and clue if you feel that you are neither in control of your future or your life. James Allen in his fine book, *As a Man Thinketh*, says: "They themselves are makers of themselves." Your success is not determined by your external environment but your reaction or adjustment to that environment. Your success has nothing to do with your age, sex, color, the interest rate, the economy, the company you represent or the state or territory in which you sell. Your success has to do more with your internal mental environment than your external physical surroundings. Albert Gray, a number of years ago, did a study of successful people and came up with a very enlightening finding. He studied all types of people. His goal was to find the common denominator of success. His definition, after years of study:

> *Successful people are successful because they form the habit of doing those things that failures don't like to do.*
>
> —Albert Gray

Let's evaluate that statement. What are the things that successful people do? How are they different from the things that those who fail won't do? They're not! The things are the same. The difference is that successful people do them and failures don't.

Research over the years has indicated that only 5 percent of the population can really retire at age sixty-five—that is, not be dependent on anyone or have to reduce their standard of living. (See Figure 2-G) Do you think you can become financially independent following your natural likes and dislikes? Natural tendencies? Or prejudices? Or doing what you want to do or like to do when you want to do it? If that were possible, 100 percent of the population would be financially successful. Since the actual number is only 5 percent, the truth would seem to be that you can't become financially secure following natural likes, dislikes, or tendencies.

Mr. Gray found that successful people were motivated by the pleasure of achieving results, and those who failed were motivated by comfortable methods. Successful people did many things they didn't like to do in order to get the things they wanted to get. Failures want these same things but won't do the things necessary to get them. They're motivated by comfortable methods. Ask yourself how many things are you willing to go without in your life because you don't like to do the things that, if done, would get them for you? It is sometimes easier to adjust yourself to the hardships of a poor living than to the hardships of doing things that you don't like to do.

Figure 2-G

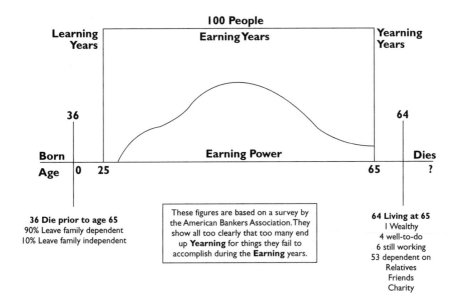

100 People

Learning Years   **Earning Years**   **Yearning Years**

36   64

Born   **Earning Power**   **Dies**

Age   0   25   65   ?

36 Die prior to age 65
90% Leave family dependent
10% Leave family independent

These figures are based on a survey by the American Bankers Association. They show all too clearly that too many end up **Yearning** for things they fail to accomplish during the **Earning** years.

64 Living at 65
1 Wealthy
4 well-to-do
6 still working
53 dependent on
Relatives
Friends
Charity

What Is a Sales Slump?

A practical example of this idea is the problem of a sales slump. A sales slump is nothing more than a period of time (either short or long) in your sales career when you are temporarily motivated by comfortable methods rather than results. Our lives are a series of highs and lows, peaks and valleys. This is especially true in sales because of the nature of both the profession and your natural tendency to feel you deserve a short break after a successful sale, a productive day, or a prosperous month. (See Figure 2-H)

While you are moving toward your sales objective, the goal or result is what motivates you. When you achieve the goal, you relax for a short time. If that relaxation time continues long enough, many of us fall into a habit that is comfortable for us. It isn't until we reach a bottom point that we again begin to do the things we should do to achieve the success or results we desire. One of the best things you can do for a successful sale or day is to transmit the attitudes, enthusiasm, and confidence you have gained from success and direct them into another telephone call or personal visit. By all means don't lose the value of the momentum that you have gained. When you're hot…you're hot!

Figure 2-H

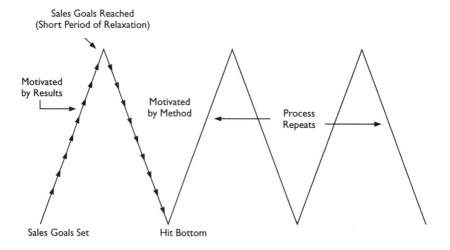

Success is a lot like happiness. Happiness is not something that is a goal in and of itself. Happiness is a by-product of an internal peace and harmony when everything in the world seems right. People who are trying to find happiness outside themselves are never happy. Happiness for them is always someplace where they're not or something they don't have—a new car, another drink, a new job, another home, retirement, next year's vacation, a new spouse. Happy is where you are right now. If you are not happy as you read this book, when you put it down for another activity one thing is still unchanged...YOU! You take you wherever you go and into every activity you are involved with. You must spend all your life with yourself. There will be other friends, relatives, associates who will come and go, but you will always be with you. Learn that happiness is an internal not an external thing.

And so is success. It is what's within you, not your physical, personal, or psychological exterior or environment. Success is a quiet, internal, personal journey. It speaks not by words and deeds, but by what you are and become as you move along life's journey. The goal of most modern millionaires was not money, but to provide a better product or service. Their financial reward was a natural by-product of their creative genius, faith, enthusiasm and hard work. Read that time-tested piece of literature, *Acres of Diamonds* by Russell Conwell. Its very simple message is that your success may very well be right where you are standing, living or working, and not someplace else. Success, happiness and fortune is where you are. It starts with you. The success journey begins with you and in you when you decide on your direction in life. This journey never ends.

There are as many nights as days and the one is just as long as the other in the year's course. Even a happy life cannot be without a measure of darkness, and the word "happy" would lose its meaning if it were not balanced by sadness. It is far better to take things as they come along with patience and equanimity.

—Carl Jung

What is Motivation?

Over the years, reams of material and tremendous amounts of effort and research have gone into the concept of motivation. Parents, teachers, sales managers, coaches, and many others have been plagued by a lack of motivation and productivity in individuals. It seems to me, however, that understanding the idea of motivation is not as difficult as much of the research would indicate. The word motivation means "induce, move, draw on, give an impulse to, inspire, prompt, stimulate, rouse, incite, instigate, sway, tempt, provoke, inspirit, influence." (These terms really are helpful, aren't they?) *Webster's* goes on: "Something that causes a person to act." Well, I think that is the heart of the matter. Let's look at the practical aspect of the word. Break it up—MOTIVATION—now put an 'E' after the 'V' and a 'C' after the 'A.' Now what have you? MOTIVE/ACTION. Yes, it's quite simple. Motivation is goal-directed action. Action towards a purpose, goal or objective. If you can recall what our definition of success was earlier in this chapter—moving towards a predetermined, personal goal—the two ideas are very similar. If you have motivation, you have success. But you can't have success with only half of the word. For example, "Today, I will have action but no motives," or, "Today, I will have the motives but no action." Both ingredients are necessary.

It has taken me the better part of more than 20 years of personal research and study to develop the following understanding. The key to your ultimate success is hidden in motive/action. It's your ability to maintain a high degree of internal motivation, to have both motives and actions on a daily basis.

When studying the lives of successful people, Mr. Gray found that he could not just look at what they did but also what made them do it. Napoleon Hill in his legendary research on success found that the starting point of all achievement was a "definite major purpose." Before you can take action you must have goals. But once you have the goals, you then must take action. Later in this chapter we will discuss goal-setting in greater detail. Let us talk about each part of the definition.

Have you ever said: "Someday honey…;" "I've got a half a mind to…;" "I'm going to…;" "When the conditions are right…"? Many times the motive part of the concept of motivation is the easier of the two. Let's take a look at the action portion.

How do we move ourselves or others; how do we motivate? One common misconception I would like to clear up now is the notion that you can motivate others. You cannot motivate anyone but yourself. I am amazed at the number of sales managers and supervisors who ask me, "How do you motivate people?" You don't motivate people, you show them how to motivate themselves and turn the responsibility of motivation over to each of them. When you attend a seminar, read a motivational book, or listen to a motivational cassette, it can cause, over a short period of time, stimulated activity or increased temporary success. Usually this is caused by a degree of excitation or stimulation. But I repeat, normally the results of this kind of short-lived exposure are very temporary. And this is really not motivation if we look at the concept of "goal-directed action."

Motivation is not an external factor, but an internal one. Parents don't motivate their children, sales managers don't motivate their salespeople; people motivate themselves. Management's only responsibility in the motivation of its employees is to establish a favorable climate where people can want to or know how to motivate themselves. Everyone is motivated to one degree or another. Even the motivation to do nothing is motivation. The motive: to do nothing; the action: meaningless behavior.

Everyone is motivated! The employee who is always late is more motivated by sleeping late than being on time.

The common external or historical methods of motivation are fear and incentives. Both are external. They are a force outside themselves, and therefore have a tendency to be very temporary. Let's look at the oldest form of motivation first.

> But what is happiness except the simple harmony between a
> man and the life he leads?
>
> —Albert Camus

Fear Motivation

Fear motivation for many is effective. The major problem with fear motivation is that it doesn't work all the time on everybody. The main reason is because it is based on the wrong element. It is based on punishment—the idea of "do it or else." If the individual is willing to tolerate the punishment, then fear motivation will not be effective. With repeated use of fear motivation people have a tendency to raise their tolerance to the threat itself. For example, "Reach your quota this month or you're fired!" If the salesperson doesn't care if he's fired, it won't get him to reach his quota. "Get that report in to me by Friday or you don't need to continue to work here." If the person or individual doesn't care whether he or she continues to work there, than that is not going to get them to complete the report on time. The same problem can be illustrated with children. "Honey, if you don't get the dishes done, you cannot go out after dinner." If he or she doesn't care whether he goes out after dinner, the threat will not motivate him or her to do the dishes. So the problems with fear motivation are that it is temporary, it is negative and it is based on the wrong thing.

Incentive Motivation

The opposite of fear motivation is reward or what we call incentive motivation. You would think that incentive motivation or money motivation would be more effective than fear motivation because it appears to be the opposite. And indeed, it is somewhat more effective. But it still has its inherent problems. It is also temporary. Incentive motivation is temporary because it is also based on the wrong element. Incentive motivation or reward motivation is based on a want, and once a want is satisfied, it is no longer a want and no longer serves to motivate. To continue to motivate the individual you must raise the want level. A good example would be a sales contest where the first prize is a color television. If everyone in the company participating in the contest already owns two color televisions, the sales results probably wouldn't increase much. If the reward was a four-week vacation around the world, there might be increased enthusiasm or there might be temporarily increased productivity as a result of that type of reward. So the productivity, then, is related to the reward or the want of a reward by the individual.

Figure 2-I
THE TYPES OF MOTIVATION

FEAR MOTIVATION   INCENTIVE MOTIVATION

One good way to look at incentive motivation is to be aware that a number of years ago, a major consulting organization did some research on executive compensation. It found that in order to motivate top executives with money, companies had to inject it into their compensation package in massive doses. In other words, take top executives earning $250,000 a year and offer them $10,000 a year to do more, and the executives response was, "Who needs it!" To get them to do more, companies had to offer $50,000, $75,000, or $100,000 in additional income.

If we look at the bottom of the economic ladder where there are literally tens of thousands of people on unemployment or welfare, the problem is the same. Their needs and wants are satisfied on $150 per week. Why should they go out and get a job that pays only $10 a week more than the welfare check? Only if there is a substantial increase in income will the person be motivated by reward motivation, and then only if he or she is dissatisfied with their current existence. So here we have the bottom to the top of the economic ladder basing productivity on reward.

Picture in your mind, if you will, a donkey harnessed to a cart loaded with dirt. In front of the donkey is a stick with a bunch of carrots dangling from it. This will work. The donkey will pull the cart chasing the carrots as long as certain conditions are met. For example, the cart must be light enough and stable. The donkey must be hungry enough and like carrots. The carrots must be big enough and fresh, and the stick must be long enough, yet short enough. If all of these conditions are met, the donkey will chase the carrots and pull the cart. (See Figure 2-I)

However, we are not donkeys. You recognize the significance of the stick. Your thought is, I can chase these carrots all day long and pull this cart and never get a bite. So to make this formula work on a human being, we must every now and then give them a bite of the carrot, or an incentive or reward. Once we have done that we have altered one of the primary conditions of our formula, which is the hunger of the donkey, or individual. In order to have the system continue to be effective, we must continue to offer the donkey or individual a larger bite and more frequently. The interesting thing is we must also lighten the load. Many times when you give employees a raise they don't necessarily do more because of that raise. Many times they actually do significantly less because they feel they have deserved the raise and it is not necessarily a requirement to do more, but to relax.

One of the inherent problems in the sales profession is that many companies use a combination of both fear and incentives to motivate their people. These two systems, however, have been moderately effective over the years at getting average productivity. Organizations and individuals must recognize that the best method of motivation is not external, but internal. In other words, let's get the donkey to pull the cart because he wants to pull the cart, not because we threaten him or because we reward him with carrots. This type of motivation works well with people as opposed to donkeys.

Why Salespeople Fail

There are a number of reasons why people fail in sales. There are probably as many reasons why people fail in sales as there are salespeople who have failed. I realize you might think that this is not a very profound statement, but the reasons individuals fail are individual reasons. In this section I will attempt to cover the major reasons why people fail in sales. I believe that in order to establish good habits—good selling habits—we need to know not only our weaknesses, but our strengths. You may recall that at the end of chapter one I asked you to complete the self-analysis questionnaire. One of the items was a rather close and honest look at both your strengths and weaknesses. The following list represents why most people fail in sales. Carefully analyze yourself in each area (see Figure 2-J). Rate yourself on a scale of one to ten.

Poor planning. It is amazing how little salespeople plan their activities, their days, their sales calls, or their lives. They will travel halfway across town and waste three hours to get to a poorly-qualified prospect and in the meantime, pass dozens of prospects within walking distance of their home or office. Or they will enter into a sales situation without having given the prospect or the sales call adequate thought, preparation or planning. Ask yourself, "On Friday, do I know what I will be doing every day next week, or do I wait until Monday to decide what I will do on Monday? When I crawl into bed on Tuesday night, do I know exactly what I will be doing on Wednesday, or do I wait until I get to the office on Wednesday to determine what I will do on Wednesday?" Planning is an important part of your success in the sales profession—planning your time, planning your calls, and planning all of your selling activities. Most of the successful salespeople I have known spend more time in pre-call preparation and planning than they do in the actual sales session or interview. Most of the losers that I have known in sales spend most of their times in the sales interviews and very little time in sales planning.

Poor attitude. People fail in sales continuously because they cannot control their own attitudes. What do I mean by controlling your attitude? Let me give you an illustration. You have just finished your fourth sales call of the day, your fourth rejection of the day. It is 3:00 p.m. and you have an appointment at 3:30. If you're a pro, you enter into that situation with the same positive attitude you had during your first appointment of the day. Very few people have that kind of control. You must separate each sales call, each sales event, each rejection and think of it in separate terms. Your ability to control your attitude on a daily basis is proof of your success in this profession. You need to train your mind to react to the negatives—the problems, the criticisms, the failures—no differently than you would the success in your sales day.

Being ignorant is not so much a shame as being unwilling to learn.
—Ben Franklin

Lack of continuous training. Nearly two hundred years ago during the administration of President Adams, the U.S. Patent Office came within three votes of being closed because officials thought everything worthwhile had been invented. One of the problems with people today, especially salespeople, is that they have closed their patent offices. Some rather interesting research I read recently indicates the average individual invests several hundred dollars per year on the outside of his or her head and body to improve appearance—haircuts, shaving cream, perfume, makeup and clothes. The same average individual spends several thousand dollars for an automobile, plus at least $20-$30 more per week to get them to and from prospects' offices or homes. Let's summarize. If you're like the average individual just mentioned, you have invested at this point several thousand dollars to make you look good, smell good and get you in front of your prospects. My question to you is, "What did you invest last year on the inside of your head so you would know what to say when you got there?"

Most of the people who need sales training today don't take it. Their attitude is, "I took the Dale Carnegie course fifteen years ago, read a sales book 10 years ago and bought a cassette one time—there's nothing new. I'm not going to hear anything from this individual that I haven't already heard." Most of the people who have attended my classes have not been the losers in sales, but the winners. It's been my experience that the people who need training never take it. The people who are successful are successful primarily because of their attitude toward self-improvement. They are always buying books, attending seminars, taking courses, listening to cassettes, and attending meetings to improve themselves.

Poor use of time. You and I got up this morning with one common denominator in our journey toward success. We were both given 24 hours. Whether you are twenty, thirty or fifty years old, you have had the same amount of time to become successful or unsuccessful as your neighbor or associates of equal age. The key to success is not how much time you have, but how you use your time each day. It has been my experience that people in sales who regularly abuse their time seldom accomplish much for themselves, their families, or their clients. The successful salespeople are time-conscious. They realize every minute of the day is a potential for income. They think creatively, they sell creatively, they improve themselves creatively, they even dream creatively through the skills of auto-suggestion and visualization. In this section, there are several forms or charts which I recommend you use to analyze how you use your time, both positively and negatively. (See Figures 2-N through 2-R) These will help you improve the use of your time.

Lack of specific goals. We will, in this chapter, go into greater detail on goal-setting and its value. At this point I would just like to mention that if you don't know where you're going, that's probably the reason you're not getting there. But if you do have a clear-cut specific plan for success for your life, then you probably are achieving your objective fairly near the schedule you have set for yourself. One of the differences between successful people and unsuccessful people is their purpose in life—their goals. If we look at the word motivation (and we agreed that motivation means the same thing as success), then half of our success is going to be determined by our goals. The lack of goals will determine the lack of our success.

Lack of self-discipline. Self-discipline is an integral quality that gets you to do things long after the commitment, the enthusiasm, or the decision to do those things has past. For example, let's say that after completing this chapter you decide to experiment with several of the time-management exercises we have suggested and four weeks from now you are no longer doing what you said you would do. Instead, you did it the next day because the momentum, the decision, the enthusiasm surrounding the decision was immediate. Self-discipline gets you to continue to do the things you said you would do long after that initial commitment or that enthusiasm has gone.

Procrastination. Do you have the habit of procrastination? Can you carry the enthusiasm, commitment, dedication, and action into both pleasant and unpleasant tasks?

If you don't act or make a decision, you know the outcome. Nothing will change; it will be as it is. But if you make a new decision, take off in an unpleasant or unknown direction—fear develops. Procrastination is fear of the unknown. If you have a fear, do the thing you fear and you will overcome your fear.

Lack of concentration. You must be able to focus 100 percent of your attention on your prospect. I don't care if you have marital, financial or personal problems. You must force them out of your mind while trying to sell. The prospect should be the center of your world, and deserves your best at all times.

Neglecting self-evaluation and appraisal. Why is it that people who need self-evaluation the most never seem to ask? The winners in sales constantly ask their customers, prospects, managers, associates, or spouses, "What can I do to improve?" They are not afraid of criticism, they encourage it.

Inability to cope with rejection. This is the major cause of failure in sales. We'll discuss this problem in greater detail later in this chapter.

Inability to fail. Sales is a failing business. Invariably, if you are seeing enough people and making enough calls, you will have a high percentage of failures. What will determine your success in sales more than any other fact is your ability to fail successfully and keep trying, learning, and improving.

Lack of creative imagination. Are you still trying to sell the same way you did last year? Are you selling each prospect the same way? Do you sell the same way every day? If your success depended on your creative approach to each new prospect each day, how would you be doing?

These are the major causes of failure in sales. Throughout this book we will go into great detail on how to avoid or overcome these negative traits or habits. For now, be aware that they exist and assess if you are in jeopardy.

Figure 2-J
Evaluate Yourself in These Important Areas Now!

	Your Self-Rating	Other Rating	Difference In Two Ratings
Poor planning —			
Poor attitude —			
Lack of continuous training —			
Poor use of time —			
Lack of specific goals —			
Lack of self-discipline —			
Procrastination —			

Lack of concentration —

Neglecting self-evaluation and appraisal —

Inability to cope with rejection —

Inability to fail —

Lack of creative imagination —

Important success qualities

Tomorrow every fault is to be amended—but that tomorrow never comes.
—Ben Franklin

The following twenty qualities are generally found in most successful salespeople. Not all salespeople exhibited all twenty—or exhibited them to the same degree. The entire list, however, represents all the qualities that were found. Again, why not rate yourself on the same 1–10 scale and ask another associate, manager or spouse to rate you (obviously without access to your own evaluation). (See Figure 2-K)

Definiteness of purpose. All achievement begins with a clear, well-defined purpose. The strength of your purpose is what will determine your ultimate success.

Desire. Desire is the equalizer that will make up for a lack of many of the other qualities, if you have enough of it. Desire keeps you going. Desire comes from within, not without. Set yourself on fire with desire for the things you want in life.

Enthusiasm. Emerson said: "Nothing of consequence was ever accomplished without enthusiasm." It is the spark of achievement. You don't necessarily become enthusiastic when you are successful—but you can become successful because of your enthusiasm. Enthusiasm is a quiet confidence. The word comes from the Greek word "entheos," meaning "from God." Enthusiasm doesn't have to be loud or boisterous. Enthusiasm comes from confidence; confidence comes from knowledge;

knowledge comes from experience; and experience comes from confrontation. You learn by doing and by doing you gain experience, knowledge, confidence, and enthusiasm.

Use of knowledge. You've heard that knowledge is power. Not so. The use of knowledge is power. Knowledge is worthless if you don't use it and difficult to use if you don't have it. Put only that information in your head which can be of use to you. Then use it when necessary. Surround yourself with the people who have the information you need.

Self-confidence. Self-confidence is an inner power and strength that is generated from ability, action and knowledge. These give you productivity.

Pleasing personality. Are you the kind of person you would like to be around? What ingredients constitute a pleasing personality? Sincerity, warmness, friendliness, happiness, congeniality, interest? Can you name any others? How many would you possess if described by a stranger? Try it!

Faith and belief. There are many things to have faith and belief in: God, yourself, your company, your product or service, your profession, the free enterprise system, your country, the future. What others would you add?

Going the extra mile. This is where we lose a lot of would-be successes. This is giving more service than is asked of you, doing more for a client, customer, employer, spouse or whomever, than he or she expects. Develop the habit of giving more than you get, not less. It's an interesting law of nature—you may not be repaid by that spouse, prospect or employer—but it will come back to you in much greater quantity than you give.

Persistence. Winston Churchill said it best: "Never give up, never, never give up."

Goal-oriented. If you don't know where you are going, it's easy not to get there. You must set and move towards goals daily.

Self-discipline. Consistently doing what you know you should rather than what you are comfortable with is not easy but it is necessary. Form the habit of doing things now.

Personal initiative. If you didn't have this trait to some degree you wouldn't have read this far—but how do you apply this in your selling? Stop for a few minutes — do you apply initiative in all areas of your life? Consistently? For example, do you regularly go the extra mile for your customers? When you get a "no" do you give up or press on? Do you try to do a little better in your selling every day? Are you content to sell the way you always have?

Imagination. It's been said that salespeople are problem-solvers. I like to take this a little further. I believe that the most successful salespeople are problem-creators. They see circumstances and situations far beyond the vision of the average salesperson. They then create a problem to be solved. This takes imagination and creativity.

Concentration. Your ability to focus or concentrate your attention and actions on the task, problem or prospect at hand is not only necessary but extremely valuable to the success of the sales process. It shows interest, concern, and true mental self-discipline.

Positive self-image. Your self-image is your internal gyroscope. It has been preset by your conditioning environment and the beliefs you've formed about yourself and your abilities. It can be reset if it is negative. A negative self-image will generally cause low self-esteem, lack of confidence, low achievement, weakened drive, and inferiority tendencies—none of which will aid your career in sales.

Learning from defeat. Adversity, failure, and defeat are the best teachers if we will only learn from them. According to Napoleon Hill, "Every adversity, heartbreak or setback brings with it the seed of an equivalent or greater benefit." But you have to pick the defeat or failure apart. The lesson is not going to jump out at you. But, it is usually there, well-hidden, if you look.

Sound health. What good is it to be the most successful salesperson in your company, but have an ulcer, or the most successful salesperson in your industry, but drop dead at age 40 from a heart attack? Good health is an important aspect of success. Without it, can you enjoy your success?

Budget your time and money. There is one sure way to guarantee your economic security. Save and invest 10 percent of all you earn. No matter how much or how little it may be. Form the habit of saving 10 percent regularly. The amount is not what's important. It's the habit that counts. For salespeople, time is money. Ten percent of your time should be invested in your own self-improvement. You should also invest 5 percent of your yearly income in your future. You can't afford not to. Your competition is.

Accurate thinking. Refine your ability to see people as they are, not as they would like you to see them. The ability to see situations and problems as they are, not as you would like them to be. It's your ability to cut through to the core of a problem quickly without undue pressure from your environment.

Empathy. I don't believe you can succeed as a parent, manager, or salesperson with sympathy. You must have empathy. What is the difference? Sympathy is the inclination to think or feel like another person, to put yourself in their shoes, so to speak. Empathy is the ability to understand how another person is feeling, but not feeling the way they feel.

The prospect says, "I can't afford it." If you also couldn't afford it, the tendency is to feel sympathy and say, "You're probably right, I'll check back with you next month, year, etc." With empathy you understand how they feel, but don't put yourself in their place. Let's say you are the type of person that has to think something over before you buy. Your prospect now says, "I have to think it over." Again, if that's the way you are, sympathy gets in your way, and you'll let him think it over. Unfortunately, most of us have been raised to show sympathy, not empathy. With sympathy, you may make a few temporary friends, but few sales. Empathy helps you help people to help themselves. Sympathy prevents growth and encourages dependency.

When you have these twenty qualities, you have character, integrity, emotional maturity, success, and the potential for greatness.

Figure 2-K
Qualities Necessary for Success

	Your Self-Rating	Other Rating	Difference In Two Ratings
Definiteness of purpose—			
Desire—			
Enthusiasm—			
Use of knowledge—			
Self-confidence—			
Pleasing personality—			
Faith and belief—			

Going the extra mile—

Persistence—

Goal-oriented—

Self-discipline—

Personal initiative—

Imagination—

Concentration—

Positive self-image—

Learn from defeat—

Sound health—

Budget time and money—

Accurate thinking—

Empathy—

The Purpose of Goal-setting

Ralph Waldo Emerson said: "The world makes way for the man who knows where he is going." The tragedy is that so few know where they are going. According to social scientists, less than 5 percent of the population have ever taken the time to think about specific goals they would like to achieve.

The joy we experience from living is not in being complete, but in becoming complete. We are always in the process, and if we have begun to take charge of our lives, that process is one of growth. To be sure that we are growing rather than merely moving, we have to take time to reflect on where we are moving and assess how far we have come. Without a conscious recognition of a destination, our journey through life can be little more than aimless wandering. With a clear notion of where we are going, our journey becomes self-directed and our actions become meaningfully related to the goal of arriving at our destination.

We formulate our destination in terms of long-term goals. Once we have determined where we choose to be in the distant future (ten years, twenty years from now), we can then concern ourselves with how we are to arrive there and what are to be the significant points along the way (short-term goals). If we have mapped out our goals, we will be able to look at our compass anywhere along the route to be sure that we are not getting side-tracked. We will also be noticing all the interesting scenery around us, enjoying the journey, and possibly discovering that there are other destinations to which we may choose to go. Goal-setting is not a one-time process, but a continual one in which goals are re-evaluated and new goals are set.

Finally, we must distinguish clearly between goals on the one hand, and wishes, hopes, and dreams on the other. With goals, we live in the present and work toward the achievement of a goal-directed future. With wishes, hopes and, dreams we may forget to live in the present and attempt to live in a nonexistent future. Life is about the now.

Establishing Goals

Webster's defines a goal as: "The end toward which effort is directed." Effective goals should have the following characteristics: they are written, measurable, positive, worthwhile, and inclusive of every area of one's life.

Just as an organization has many necessary functions to perform to support its overall organizational mission (e.g., accounting, data processing, marketing, manufacturing, personnel), we human beings have many areas of our lives that need to be functioning well if we are to achieve our mission of being happy and productive. Setting a goal for ourselves to be experts in accounting will be of little avail if we don't also set goals to enjoy physical health, to make enough money to cover the costs of our training, to develop people skills so we can market our talents, etc. A happy, well-balanced life is one in which goals are being realized in every area.

Most people spend more time planning a party or a vacation than they do planning their lives. And then they wonder why they have to go without many of the good things of life.

Most people say they have goals, but in reality those "goals" are little more than daydreams or vague desires.

We already have discussed the importance of goals as they affect your motivation. Now, let's look at the "how to's" of goals.

You've heard it said that you have to have goals. Deep in your heart you believe it yet, as you read, you have not done what you know you should have done in this area. So let's get to it.

Goal-setting is really a very simple exercise if you just break it down into a series of short steps.

Some General Guidelines

Tangible and intangible goals. Tangible goals are the physical things you want to get or have (a new car, for example). Intangible goals are usually personality characteristics you want to obtain or something you want to become (for example, more self-disciplined, enthusiastic).

Many times the reasons why we do not reach our tangible goals is because we have not set and reached the intangible goals first. The reasons why you don't have the new car is because you may lack self-discipline and until you overcome this, the new car may not be a realistic goal.

Short-term vs. Long-term Goals

Short-term to me is less than six months: today, this week, this month. Long-term is a year, five years, or a lifetime. Stop now and complete the following exercises:

A.   In less than twenty-five words, what is your major purpose in life?

B.   What do you want in life? Dream—Where do you want to visit?

What do you want to become? What do you want to have? List as many items as you can before going on.

One of the problems many people have in goal-setting is that they have been conditioned for many years not to want, so by age 20–25 we don't believe we deserve success or its trappings. According to Dorothea Brande in her book *Wake Up and Live*, we have all been programmed to fail and most of us follow this programming to the letter, to our death. The program can be changed, but it takes a great deal of persistent, conscious action.

Goals Must Be Personal and Worthwhile

You can't get excited about someone else's goal for you. Your goals must be yours in order to create the internal drive to strive forward.

Your Goals Should Stretch You a Little

They should also be realistic and attainable. Setting the goals too high many times prevents you from the small short-term successes that you need to build your confidence for the bigger, more stretching goals. For example, your last year's income was $15,000. You just entered the sales profession and your first year's goal is $100,000 income. It's possible, but highly unlikely.

Goal-setting is a habit that can take months to implement properly. Your goals must create desire for you; they must literally set you on fire. And your goals must be written. Writing down your goals crystallizes your thinking and helps you believe your goals are attainable.

How to Set Goals

Step I: Plan to spend a few hours alone some evening without interruptions. Take a legal pad and just dream a little. Put down on paper everything you've ever wanted to do, have, or become. Be careful here. There is a strong tendency to only set goals that are within your current education, age, experience, or finances. For example, you want to be president of your company, but you are only a production assistant and you have just joined the company. You think— "I don't have the experience or the knowledge," so you don't set the goal. In other words, you prejudge your future ability to achieve based on your present circumstances, income, conditions, or surroundings.

Don't prejudge. At this point the goals need not be realistic. The purpose of this step is to get your imagination moving after many years of being semi-dormant. Just let yourself dream.

There is a concept is psychology called right- and left-brain thinking. It is generally believed that the left (dominant) half of your brain is responsible for logical thought, reasoning, and anything involving language. The right half, in contrast, is considered to control artistic creativity and intuitive thinking or imagination.

For the most part, the right half has not been developed as much as the left. Through our years of education and childhood we were not encouraged to think and create, but rather to memorize and obey. This is unfortunate, because it is this right half where we dream and imagine. It can guide the left half to productive activity. This exercise is to get the sand or cobwebs out of your imagination. Don't worry about realism during this step. Just dream!

Step II: Take the list of dreams you've made—let's call it your master goal list. Create seven new lists. Each of the items in this master list will probably fall into one of the following categories: mental, physical, social, financial, spiritual, business, and family. Just break down the master list into seven. Don't worry if you end up with fifteen items in one category and none in another. Just separate.

Step III: Prioritize each list. Look at each list separately without regard for any other list. Ask yourself which item on the list is most important, then second, third and so on. You should now have seven categories (even if you have nothing listed under the category, be sure to write all seven categories) with all the most important things to you at the top of each list.

Step IV: Now look at each number one—are these things the most important to you now? Keep in mind that your values are constantly changing. What was important to you at age twenty-five is not necessarily what's important to you at age fifty or seventy. Now choose the most important number one from each category.

Step V: Now plug each goal you have selected into the work-sheet provided in Figure 2-L. Next, set a target date and define the goal. It must be stated positively. Let's say you weigh two hundred pounds. A goal to lose twenty pounds is stated negatively. Positively stated, it would read, "I want to reach 180 pounds."

Step VI: Move progressively through the worksheet. One more word of caution. It takes just as much time to become an accomplished goal-setter as it does to develop any other new skill. Don't be impatient. Recognize that your progress will be slow in the beginning. As you become more proficient, not only will it be easier, but you will begin to accomplish goals and tasks you once thought unrealistic.

Affirmations and Visualization

To initiate the reprogramming of our subconscious minds so that we overcome the self-limitations imposed upon and perpetuated by us, we need to create a fundamental affirmation for each area of our life to serve as a foundation for greater achievement. Your success in programming your mind for success depends on the faithfulness with which you practice this process. Three times a day is the absolute minimum.

Once the foundation for success has been laid (after three weeks), you are ready to add to your fundamental affirmations your own specific affirmations derived from your long-term and short-term goals in each of the seven areas of your life. A goal is a future event; an affirmation, a vividly imagined "present" experience.

Visualizing goals is the key to attaining them. Nothing is realized in the realm of external reality until it is realized in the internal realm of your mind and imagination.

Creating Affirmations

In Figure 2-M, write down your most important long-term goal in each of the seven areas of your life. Then, write down one short-term goal for each of the long-term goals. Finally, translate each of the goals into affirmations by using the present tense and emphasizing the present nature of the event by using such words as "enjoy," "admire," or "see." For example, the goal to make $100,000 a year in salary might translate into the affirmation, "I enjoy the lifestyle that my $100,000-a-year salary enables me to have." The goal of losing twenty pounds becomes, "I admire the shapeliness of my 180-pound body."

Figure 2-L

Goal-Setting Worksheet

Date Worked on:_____   Type of Goal:_____ Term:_____

                                    (Tangible or intangible)   (Short or long)

Life Area:_____   Target Date:_____

        (Mental, physical, financial, family, career, spiritual or social)

Goal or objective   Must be specific and written positively_____

Obstacles or problems   Why don't I have it now?_____

Possible Solutions   Is it worth it to me?_____

Action Steps; things I will do   How serious am I?_____

Benefits I will receive   What will it mean to me when I accomplish this goal?_____

Feedback or schedule of progress_____

Figure 2-M

	Goals	Affirmation

Mental   Long-Range Goals _____
              Short-Range Goals

Physical Long-Range Goals _____
              Short-Range Goals

Financial Long-Range Goals _____
              Short-Range Goals

Family   Long-Range Goals _____
              Short-Range Goals

Career   Long-Range Goals _____
              Short-Range Goals

Spiritual Long-Range Goals _____
              Short-Range Goals

Social   Long-Range Goals _____
              Short-Range Goals

Visualizing Your Fundamental Self-affirmations

Man is condemned to be free; because once thrown into the world, he is responsible for everything he does.

—Jean Paul Sartre

While reciting your self-affirmations, whether the fundamental seven or the specific personal ones, you must visualize and/or deeply feel the experience of success, remembering that the brain cannot distinguish between real experience and deeply imagined, intensely felt experience. The more vividly you imagine and the more intensely you feel the experience, the more quickly you will attain the fundamental positive outlook and the specific goals you have set.

Going into deep relaxation before the visualizing process is akin to the dimming of the lights in a movie theater before the film begins. The more deeply relaxed, the more vividly you are able to visualize.

Sample self-affirmations

1. I admire the physical extension of me—what I call my body—and I nourish, strengthen, and protect it, even as I would nourish, strengthen, and protect _____. (Add the name of a loved one here.)

2. I enjoy the special way I have of relating to others and the special ways others have of relating to me.

3. I marvel at how capable my mind is of assimilating, analyzing, synthesizing, and remembering everything to which I have become exposed.

4. I see my life as the gradual unfolding of a hidden agenda, in which each career position is preparing me to assume greater and greater responsibility, and is providing me with further opportunities to excel and contribute.

5. I am proud of my ability to provide for my own needs and those of others, and I view money as a positive means of achieving freedom and independence of action.

6. I know how important it is to play, and I always allow myself the opportunity to experience the pleasure and relaxation that recreation provides.

7. I become more and more aware of the significance of my thoughts, words and actions. I become increasingly confident that they have a deeper meaning than I can yet fully appreciate.

Procedure for Reading Self-affirmations

1. Allow yourself to experience deep relaxation by slowly counting from 1–20, imagining yourself becoming more and more relaxed with each count.
2. Picture in your mind a spot where you can be deeply relaxed (e.g., a beach, a field of flowers, a hot tub) and concentrate on all the sights, sounds, smells, tastes, and tactile images associated with that place.
3. When you first begin doing the exercises, read each affirmation and then repeat it three times with your eyes closed. When you have memorized your affirmations, keep your eyes closed throughout and recite in your "mind's ear" each affirmation three times.
4. Visualize and vividly imagine supporting experiences that help to confirm the reality of the affirmation you are reciting.
5. When you have completed all your affirmations, spend a few more moments relaxing in the spot you have chosen to visualize and then count slowly back to alertness from 20–1, becoming gradually more alert (but still relaxed) with each count.
6. After reading your fundamental self-affirmations three times a day for three weeks, you are ready to add to them more specific affirmations derived from your individual goals (ten maximum).

Inducing a State of Deep Relaxation

When you first begin the deep relaxation process, you will require several minutes to consciously relax. With experience, the process will occur almost instantaneously. Below is a "narrative" that may be helpful for those who are just beginning the process:

You are going to experience a state of deep relaxation. Check to be sure that your legs are planted firmly on the floor (not crossed), and that your arms are resting comfortably on your lap or on the arms of your chair. Sit up straight in your chair, but not rigidly. Closing your eyes, I want you to focus your attention on your feet. Lift the right foot off the ground, feel the tension in your leg, drop it and feel how heavy and relaxed your right leg is. Now lift your left foot off the ground, feel the tension in your leg, drop it and feel how heavy and relaxed it is. Lift both arms a couple of inches, feel the tension, drop them and feel how heavy they feel. Lean forward two inches, feel the slight discomfort, fall back heavily into the chair. Let your chin drop to your chest and let your head slowly rotate until it comes back to center, and assumes its natural position. Now, scrunch your face as tight as you can. Allow it to relax, feeling your jaw drop and your eyes relaxing beneath your eyelids.

Now in your "mind's ear," I want you to count with me from 1–20. Imagine that with each count you are going deeper and deeper into the valley of relaxation and peace. 1, 2, 3 (you are beginning to relax), 4, 5 (you feel yourself sinking heavily into the chair), 6, 7, 8 (you can actually feel the relaxation slowly spreading over your body), 9, 10 (your legs feel like weights and your arms feel heavier and heavier), 11, 12, 13 (you feel your shoulders falling and any last traces of tension are leaving your body with each exhalation of air), 14, 15 (your forehead and eyes are heavier and heavier and you feel the tension leave your face with each breath, 16, 17, 18 (you are deeply relaxed and quiet, comfortable and secure), 19, 20 (you are completely relaxed as you picture in your mind's eye a setting in which you are truly happy and content, conscious of every sight, sound, smell, taste and touch associated with it).

Bringing Yourself out of Deep Relaxation

Bring yourself out of deep relaxation slowly, remembering to remain relaxed even while you are becoming more and more alert with each count. Those who have had little experience with deep relaxation may wish to model their return to alertness on the following "narrative:"

You are now becoming more and more conscious of the setting you have chosen in which you feel comfortable and secure. Enjoy this spot. Imagine that ten minutes have elapsed with each letter you hear: A, B, C, D, E, F, G. You have had a very restful time and you are anxious to return to the events of your day. With each count you will become more and more alert, more in touch with your physical surroundings. You will retain this relaxed state even as you return to alertness. Twenty, 19, 18, 17, 16 (you are becoming more aware of the world around you as you begin your ascent from the valley of relaxation and peace), 15, 14, 13, 12, 11, 10 (even though your eyes are closed, you begin to see light ahead), 9, 8, 7, 6, 5, 4 (you are reaching the top and are becoming alert to the physical environment around you), 3, 2, 1 (your eyes are open and you feel energy surging into your whole being; you express that energy by making fists with your hands). Now, taking a deep breath (in fact, yawning), you stretch your fingers and feel how rested, refreshed, and alert you are—anxious to engage in the activities that you have planned for yourself and grateful for the knowledge that you have a place to go where you can relax and build a more positive you.

Learning to be a goal-setter is like learning to drive for the first time. Recognize that is takes time and at first you will make many mistakes. But don't quit—with practice you will improve. Goal setting is the strongest force for self-motivation. Do it now.

The Truth About Failure

Every adversity, heartbreak or setback carries with it the seed
of equivalent or greater benefit.

—Napoleon Hill

See if you can recognize this dismal failure:
     —Difficult childhood
     —Less than one year formal schooling
     —Failed in business–age 31
     —Defeated for legislature–age 32
     —Again failed in business–age 33
     —Elected to legislature–age 34
     —Fiancee dies–age 35
     —Defeated for speaker–age 38
     —Defeated for elector–age 40
     —Married, wife a burden–age 42
     —Only one of four sons lived past age 18
     —Defeated for Congress–age 43
     —Elected to Congress–age 46
     —Defeated for Congress–age 48
     —Defeated for Senate–age 55
     —Defeated for Vice President–age 56
     —Defeated for Senate–age 58

When you think of a series of setbacks like this, doesn't it make you feel small to become discouraged just because you think you're having a hard time in building your business or your life? Dissatisfaction with things as they are, the persistent struggle to reach expanding goals—these are what make people great. This is the story of a man who never stopped trying even though his failures were many and his successes few. He is today one of our most beloved Americans and you will certainly know him when one more item is added: Elected U.S. President, 1860.

The "failure" was, of course, Abraham Lincoln.

Let's now look at failure from a more practical standpoint. I'd like to use the illustration of a glass of water. Picture yourself in your best outfit and I spill a glass of water on your face. I doubt if you would like me and I'm sure your attitude toward the water would not be positive.

Let's think of the water as a negative event or a failure. Now a month later you haven't had a drink of water for weeks. The event repeats—I throw the water at your face again. Your attitude toward the water would be more positive. Let's say we have a success event. Did that water ever change? What changed was your attitude toward the water. You can't control many of the things or events in your life, but you can control the attitude you take towards the things that happen to you in life.

Take a divorce, for example. One spouse says, "I can't wait to marry again." The other says, "I'll never marry again." The event was the same for both, but the attitudes were different.

Failure is not positive or negative. It is just an event. What makes the event positive or negative is your attitude towards the failure.

Do you realistically believe that you will go through the rest of your life without any further failure? Of course not. So, if you are going to continue to fail, why not take a new and more positive outlook toward it?

A man who reforms himself has contributed his full share
towards the reformation of his neighbor.
—Norman Douglas

Criticism—Rejection—Problems

Criticism, like failure, is neither negative nor positive, but how many people really want more criticism? Not many, because they look at it as negative. It's not negative, nor is it positive. It is simply an event. Neither positive nor negative. You can't control the criticism, but you can control your attitude toward it. You can choose to look at it any way you want. Looking at it positively or constructively is more profitable for you than looking at it negatively.

Some people will say, "Well, it depends on how the criticism is given." Nonsense! I can't control how it is given, but I can control how it is taken.

Problems, likewise, are neither positive nor negative. They are simply events. But do you really want more problems? I doubt it because your attitude toward problems is probably negative. They can be negative or positive. The choice is yours. You choose the attitude toward the problem or event. It can also be an opportunity. By the way, there is only one group of people in the world who don't have problems and they're all dead! Everyone living has problems. You never really out-run your problems. You only replace them with new ones from a new job, spouse, neighborhood, school, boss, or prospect.

Risk situations are also in this category. If you tried and lost, don't let it be a negative experience. Turn it into a learning experience.

Thomas Edison conducted thousands of experiments to invent the filament which would ultimately become the electric light bulb. When interviewed by a reporter and asked how he could fail so many times and keep trying, Tom's response was, "I haven't failed 10,000 times—I've found 10,000 ways that wouldn't work."

Babe Ruth not only holds the record for home runs, but he also struck out 1,330 times. He could just as easily be known as the strikeout king.

Rejection is also in this category. It is an event that is beyond your control. You can choose to look at it either positively or negatively. As a speaker, trainer and salesperson, there is always someone who won't like me—that's their problem. What are the chances that everyone you will know or meet for the rest of your life is going to like you? You're right. So stop worrying about it. Rejection is as much a part of selling as the product or service itself.

Another way to look at rejection is economically. How many rejections or failures must you go through to reach one success? You don't really get paid for the successes. You get paid to handle the failures and rejections and stay with it.

In this business we get paid for our failures, not our successes. You must fail before you can succeed. It is a necessary growth step. In fact, I'll bet if you're not failing very much you're not succeeding much either.

Your success is directly related to your failure. The way to begin to succeed more is to begin to fail more. Be careful whom you share this idea with. They may think you are crazy. Learn from your problems. Grow from your failures. Develop from your rejections. Improve from your criticisms. But look at them as positive growth opportunities. Remember the sign on my desk! "You never fail until you stop trying."

Time Management

Time is the one and only common denominator that all people, both successes and failures, have in common. We all start each day with the same twenty-four hours. How did you use your time today?

Are you completely satisfied with your use of your share? Time is money. This is more true in sales than any other profession. And yet, I've never seen so many people in one profession abuse this commodity more than in sales. We all act as if we are going to live forever. Let's say you work an average forty-hour sales week. Most salespeople are in contact with their prospects either by phone or in person less than 50 percent of the time (it's usually more like 20 to 30 percent). You also take a two-week vacation like most people. That leaves fifty weeks, multiplied by twenty hours per week, or 1,000 hours per year you are employed. If you earn $25,000 per year, your hourly income is $25. Keep that, or whatever figure it is for you, in mind for the next few minutes.

In sales there are only six areas that need your regular attention: prospecting, sales interviews, service, travel, administration and self-improvement.

Let me share with you the results of my research with salespeople over the years. Most of the poor salespeople spend their time as in Figure 2-N, and successful salespeople, Figure 2-O.

Fig. 2-N		Fig. 2-O	
(Poor Salespeople)		(Successful Salespeople)	
Prospecting	10%	Prospecting	55%
Sales presentation	23%	Sales presentation	10%
Service	15%	Service	20%
Administration	30%	Administration	5%
Travel	20%	Travel	10%
Self-improvement	2%	Self-improvement	10%

Amazing! These poor salespeople are spending half of their time administering and traveling. And for what? One-fourth of the time they're seeing the same people over and over again! And they spend virtually no time improving themselves.

Here is how the pros use their time.

You'll note here we're over 100 percent. The pro uses his travel and waiting time for self-improvement with tapes, books, etc. He also spends most of his sales time prospecting. His attitude is, "If they'll see me and know what business I'm in, they'll buy." His closing ratio is high not because he is a good closer or a great presenter, but because he is always in the presence of a highly qualified prospect. He is also quick to terminate if a "prospect" suddenly becomes a "suspect"!

Why not take a minute now and complete the questionnaires on pages 80–82. (See Figures 2-R and 2-S.) I also suggest you use the forms in Figures 2-P and 2-Q for a two-week period. The best way to improve your use of time is to know how you currently use and abuse it.

You will also notice in Figures 2-R through 2-T four time-planning exercises that can be adapted to almost any sales position. If you currently do not have any system for daily planning, I recommend you adopt one of these forms.

Maslow's Hierarchy of Needs

Abraham Maslow, with his excellent theory on psychological levels, has given the salesperson an excellent selling tool. His information, when properly understood and applied, can greatly increase your ability to read people, tailor your presentation, and save time.

Maslow's theory states that each human organism develops through a series of psychological stages or levels. The levels are not black or white, positive or negative, but periods where your activities, thoughts and emotions are dominated by the current psychological level you are in.

The first basic level is the physical or biological. This is the need for food, shelter, water, oxygen, sleep, and other fundamental biological needs.

If you have not eaten for days, your every thought, emotion, and action will be aimed at satisfying that need. But once you eat, according to Maslow, a new or higher need comes into existence. As you read, if you are concerned about your next grocery bill, rent payment, etc., then basic survival is most likely dominating your thoughts.

The second level is the need for security or safety. This is both current safety and security, but also future security and safety. This is your need for structure, familiarity, and stability. One interesting thought is, however, your security may have more to do with what you are able to give up than what you have or must keep. We spend our time accumulating material things—cars, homes, furniture—because they make us feel secure. Just lose one and watch what happens to this security. Your security is not what you have but what and who you are.

The third level is achievement. Human beings are striving, growing organisms. We need to feel as though we are accomplishing something. The day you stop growing, you begin to stagnate and die inside. Growth is necessary for a happy, peaceful, life.

The fourth level is the need for recognition. As children, you could run around the house or yard yelling: "Mom, Dad, look at me;" "Look what I can do;" "Look what I have!" As a child you needed this recognition and acceptance. Unfortunately, as an adult you cannot run around the office, the neighborhood, or meetings yelling: "Look at me;" "Look how good I am;" "Look at what I've done!" So as an adult you buy clothes, homes, automobiles, jewelry, take vacations, and join clubs that scream, "Look at me, I'm successful!" Have you checked your recognition meter lately? Most people need more recognition and stroking. You can see this in everyday human relations.

The fifth level is the need for self-acceptance or identity or self-esteem. Maslow found that this is a higher need than recognition. In other words, before I can feel really good about me, I want you to feel good about me—to accept me. Herein lies one of the fundamental problems in selling. Many times you have to say or do things that might be in the best interest of the prospect but the prospect may not like to hear it. If you are more concerned with your own recognition, and if that is the level you are on, you may have a problem. You will stop your selling short to keep this relationship friendly toward you. You will withdraw and not sell. You will have this person liking you for now, but beware! The first time he realizes he should have bought your product or service, that it was in his best interest and it is now too late, you will be amazed at how quickly you will become incompetent. You did not try hard enough to convince him. You must believe in yourself and your product or service if you are going to succeed.

The sixth and highest psychological level is the need for self-actualization. This is the healthiest a person can be psychologically. You are at your most creative, optimistic, and positive. Self-actualized people have the need to feel they are utilizing their full potential. They have a need to give back, to leave the world a better place than when they found it.

How to Use the Maslow Hierarchy in Selling

Now that we have briefly described the six psychological levels, let's relate them to selling, communicating, and persuading.

Certain product advertising is aimed directly at biological, or physical needs: mattresses, vitamins, health foods, prescription drugs, health clubs, certain clothing, and homes.

Some products appeal to our need for security or safety: insurance, banking, investments, smoke and burglar alarms, personal security systems and products, pensions, guarantees, etc.

Still other products appeal to our need for achievement: education, books, seminars, courses, trophies, plaques. Many people become active in associations because it makes them feel as though they are growing.

Other products are aimed at the need for recognition: prestige autos, membership clubs, luxury homes, designer clothing, and pens. Did you ever notice the difference between the three types of Cross pens—the chrome and the gold? The most expensive gold pen has the thinnest black tip. Why? So that people will know you have the most expensive! And where is the end when the pen is in your pocket? Much of what we buy, we buy because of what other people, even strangers, will think. "Look at me, I'm successful!"

A few products appeal to self-esteem—cosmetics and many personal items, for example. How about the L'Oreal commercial—"I'm worth it"?

And fewer products still appeal to our need for self-actualization. Our contributions to charities, associations, trusts, and memorials of many kinds help fulfill this need. Where are you now psychologically? I suggest you take a serious look at your actions and surroundings and carefully determine your present psychological level.

Once you determine your level, the next step is to realize that different people buy for different reasons—and that different features of your product or service will appeal to different people, depending on their level. For example, you sell insurance and are discussing with your prospect the future cash value benefits of a policy when he retires. The problem is that at this time he is having trouble paying his mortgage and keeping food on the table. Question: Do you think he is either hearing you or interested in the future cash value? You're on one psychological wavelength and he is on another. The only features this prospect is interested in are the ones that satisfy his current needs or problems.

We'll spend more time on this in Chapter Four. Recognize for now that these levels exist and, since we buy emotionally and not logically, you need to realize that your sales appeal must be to the emotion or psychological level that your prospect is in.

Here is an exercise. Plug the features of your product or service in each of the six levels. Why, for example, would someone buy from you if they were in the security level? The achievement level? Later in Chapter four, I'll share with you how to use this list effectively. (See Figure 2-T)

This completes our look at you, the person. You do the things you do best because of the person you are. I believe this is the most important chapter in this book! The chapters that follow will delve into selling behavior, sales techniques, and methods. But, it has been my experience in training that if your self-understanding is not adequate or your attitude is not right, you won't use the methods or skills we'll be discussing.

Figure 2-P

day_____   **DAILY TIME PLANNER**   **date**_____

Today's Date

PEOPLE TO SEE			
Time	Person	C

LETTERS TO WRITE		
Person	Number	C

LETTERS TO WRITE	
Person/Subject	C

THINGS TO DO	
	C

ITEMS TO GET	
	C

PERSONAL	
	C

C = Completed

Figure 2-Q
DAILY TIME PLANNER
date_____

HOUR	How my time was spent	Minute wasted doing what

Figure 2-R

Do I Manage My Territory Effectively?

Check your answers
Yes   No

1. Do I plan my work to prevent running around my territory in a slip-shod fashion, wasting time and expense?

2. Do I use good judgment in spending the company's money for traveling, entertainment, etc.?

3. Do I have an objective for every call?

4. Do I plan to get more interview time—less waiting and social talk time?

5. Do I go over my plans carefully the night before to determine the people I should see and the calls to make in order to curtail wasted time and motion?

6. In planning this year to make more calls, am I guided by business reasons, not permitting personal likes and dislikes, accessibility, etc., to affect my judgment?

7. Am I planning this year to make more calls, see more people, spend more time face-to-face with buyers and devote more energy to studying the problems of my customers?

8. Do I get an early start, fit my luncheon time into my day's plan and get in a full afternoon every day?

9. Do I make my luncheon plans count double by including a customer with whom company business can be discussed to advantage outside of his office?

10. Do I always make appointments with busy, important, hard-to-see people to save their time and mine?

11. If unforeseen circumstances interrupt my planned day, do I replan to include all the missed items and pick up the plan where the interruption occurred?

12. Do I review each area of my territory before leaving it, confident I am not missing an opportunity to get more business?

13. Are my reports to the home office concise, factual and of real significance—worth my time to write and my superior's time to read?

14. Am I studying my monthly performance statement and the customer record to detect where I am falling down in managing my territory?

15. Do I regularly review the sales program and requirements placed before me as a check upon my performance as manager of my territory?

16. Do I depend too much upon my superior to handle my difficult situations, and do I lack the initiative and courage to work them out?

Figure 2-S

Check List of Time-waste Inventory

1. Do I stay in bed too long in the morning?
2. Do I spend too much time reading newspapers—morning, noon, or night ?
3. Do I waste time hanging around the office in the morning?
4. Could I reduce the time spent waiting for interviews by making definite appointments in advance?
5. Am I making too many calls that don't result in interviews simply because I don't have an appointment or didn't learn in advance (by phone) that my prospect would be out or busy?
6. Do I fail to make my waiting time productive—by reading, writing, or at least thinking about something related to my work?
7. Do I stay too long on interviews or engage in too much small talk?
8. Do I spend too much time in inactivity, idleness, or daydreaming?
9. Do I take too many breaks from my work, such as stopping for coffee, going to a movie or ball game, or playing golf?
10. Do I take too much time for lunch?
11. Do I try to talk to prospects at all possible times—such as evenings, Saturdays, Sundays, and the days preceding and holidays?
12. Do I make personal visits for canvassing purposes that could be handled just as effectively over the phone?
13. Do I make too many calls on friends or others who are not prospects or who are not of any possible value in helping me accomplish my sales objectives?
14. Do I "run out to see" many customers who could be contacted just as satisfactorily by telephone?
15. Do I waste time trying to decide whom to see or call?
16. Do I waste time trying to decide what to do next?
17. Am I traveling more miles than I would if I clustered my calls?
18. Am I traveling too many places that have nothing to do with making sales?
19. Am I wasting mileage making unnecessary trips to get home at night?
20. Do I write longer letters than are really necessary?

Figure 2-T
Basic Psychological Needs

Self-actualization

Identity/self-esteem

Recognition/acceptance

Achievement

Security/safety

Survival/biological

Chapter Summary

Your real world and conscious activities today are the result of many years of conditioning, internal self-directed dialogue, and environmental exposure.

You are the sum total of millions of impressions, thoughts, and exposures.

Most of your behavior is a result of habit. Good habits equal good results; bad habits equal bad results.

You can change, but you must want to change, know how to change and take personal responsibility for any change that will take place.

To put yourself in the top 5 percent of income earners in this country, you must pattern yourself after them.

Chapter Problem

1. Your prospect is a referral from a good client. You secure the appointment. When you arrive (ten minutes late) he is in his parent ego state. What is your next step? Write out a story of what you would do or say.

Common Mistakes to Avoid

1. Thinking you know it all and have all the answers. (You probably haven't heard all the questions.)
2. Setting only long-term and tangible goals. (You must crawl before you walk.)
3. Taking rejection personally. (It has to be the other person's problem.)
4. Turning the responsibility for your self-improvement over to your company. (Your success is up to you.)

Questions

1. What is your major purpose in life?
2. Name one goal—either tangible or intangible in each of the seven major areas of your life—that you are currently working toward.
3. What motivates you?
4. What demotivates you?
5. Define failure.
6. Define enthusiasm.
7. Define self-confidence.
8. What is self-suggestion?
9. Do you regularly undergo self-evaluation?
10. What are the major qualities necessary for success?

Time: You may delay, but time will not. Lost time is never found again.
—Ben Franklin

Visualization Exercises

See yourself as a confident, enthusiastic, positive person. Practice with your eyes closed the procedures in this chapter. Use this technique to eliminate a bad habit or to create a new positive trait or habit. You can select any item from the list of twenty qualities where you scored poorly.

Exercises

1. Write out several affirmations and read them several times daily for thirty days.
2. Practice visualization techniques once a day for fifteen minutes.
3. Practice goal-setting techniques daily. Write them down and review them at the end of the day.

Chapter Affirmations

I will do the thing I fear and will overcome the fear.
I will do it now.
I am moving daily toward the accomplishment of my goals.
My definite major purpose in life is_____.
I will give more and better service than is expected of me.
Today I am a success.

You win not by chance but by preparation.

—Roger Maris

PROSPECTING

Chapter Objectives

1. Listening is better than talking.

2. Proper qualifying can improve closing.

3. Effective people-reading skills can save time.

4. Finding the dominant emotional buying motive is the key to better selling.

5. Learn how to establish and keep control.

3

Don't judge of men's wealth or piety by their Sunday appearance.
—Ben Franklin

He that would live in peace and at ease must not speak all he knows nor judge all he sees.
—Ben Franklin

How Does the Prospect See You?

There's an old sales axiom, "Other things being equal, people buy from people they like." Being on friendly terms with a customer is seldom enough to close sales, but it's a tremendously important first step. Overcoming personal antagonism is always extremely difficult, and there's almost never any justifiable reasons for creating dislike.

Once the customer likes you, she'll give you a fair hearing. If she's in the market for what you're selling, she hopes your presentation will be good enough so that she can logically channel the business your way. Strong advantages over your competition may force her to buy from you even if she doesn't like you, but she'll place the order reluctantly—and the sale will be twice as hard to make. Your answers to the questions below have much to do with whether your customer likes you.

1. Do you make it immediately evident that you like the customer? (People instinctively like people who like them, who show an interest in them.)
2. Is your attitude pleasantly respectful? (When a customer sees that you respect her, she cannot think you're stupid.)
3. Do you make a conscientious effort to find the customer's viewpoint, to learn her problems and her needs? (Your problems don't interest her, but when you show an interest in her, she begins to like you.)
4. Are you a good listener? (The salesperson who doesn't listen patiently and attentively to what the customer says isn't going to build any friendship.)
5. Do you keep eagerness to close a sale under restraint? (When such eagerness is obvious, the customer regards it as greedy self-interest on your part.)
6. Do you talk the customer's language? (she resents your talking down to her as being patronizing; she resents your talking over her head as "putting on airs.")
7. Do you avoid arguments? (Proving conclusively to a customer that she's wrong about something is a good way to kill a sale.)
8. Do you adapt the benefits you're selling to the customer's specific situation? (She doesn't like to think she's getting the same "canned" solicitations you give everyone else.)
9. Does your personal appearance get immediate acceptance? (Neither shabby nor extreme.)
10. Do you make it apparent that you appreciate the time and attention the customer is giving you, and intend to make her courtesy worth her while.

Introduction

Your key to success in selling has more to do with your prospecting ability than with any other skill. In this chapter, I would like to sell you on one thought—that your success as a salesperson is not related to your ability to give information, but rather to your ability to get information.

The most successful salespeople I know are outstanding listeners, but only average talkers. The "gift of gab" sharpies of yesterday better learn to talk less and listen more, or take my advice and retire.

You can be a master closer, give excellent presentations, have an outstanding telephone manner, present a professional appearance and represent an outstanding product or service, but fail in selling. You must have someone to talk to. On the other hand, give me a rookie and I will teach him only to prospect and I guarantee he will outsell 80 percent of the people in his company and industry who have learned all the selling techniques.

This chapter will guide you in finding and developing more and better prospects. Your success in sales depends on your ability to prospect.

The Concept of Prospecting

Why is prospecting so important? Twenty years of experience has taught me that specializing and mastering the basics of prospecting will place you at the top of your industry regardless of your age, sex or experience. It will save you time and go a long way in saving your ego.

For example, let's say your closing ratio is not what you believe is representative of your talent, time, or experience. Could it be that you don't have good prospects to begin with?

Too many salespeople today are playing the numbers game. See enough people (both good and bad prospects) and you'll sell something sooner or later to someone. The numbers game is OK if you have an ego that is hard as steel and you have all the time in the world to succeed. Admit it—most of us, I'm sure, would rather close two out of three than two out of ten or twenty, but our approach and activity are not indicative of that.

In her book *Wake Up and Live*, Dorothea Brande tells us that most of us are going out of our way subconsciously to fail. This is especially true of salespeople. How else can you account for the fact that the average salesperson today really only "logs sales calls" on a daily basis, trying to cover as much ground as possible? The pros in the profession spend better than 50 percent of their time in prospecting. The losers spend most of their time in the presentation. They're really professional visitors.

Prospecting, as defined by *Webster's*, is exploring for gold. This definition is very appropriate in relation to selling. Picture if you will a prospector who spends his time digging endless holes, only to come up a loser time and time again, versus the prospector who surveys the land and does his homework before he turns the first shovel. In selling, you can dig for gold or chase fool's gold—the choice is yours.

Asking Questions

The key to effective prospecting is the ability and willingness to ask enough of the right questions until you feel you have a bona fide prospect. In teaching sales for the past several years, I have learned that most salespeople are either reluctant to ask probing questions or don't know how or what to ask. Before you can begin asking questions, however, you must decide what kind of information you need in order to determine whether you have a prospect. Here is where I suggest you begin:

1. Develop a laundry list of the information about your average customer that gives you a "prospect profile."
2. Take your list and develop each item into a probing question, the answer to which moves you closer to establishing your prospect as a "qualified prospect."

Let's say that your company has a requirement of no less than $500,000 in annual sales to qualify as a potential customer. It also requires a credit check and a deposit with the order. Now you can proceed in one of two ways—start selling because someone will listen, or do some digging, ask some questions, and get some answers to these three questions before you even call for an appointment. If you find your prospect is OK on two of the three and decide to gamble with an appointment, then one of your first questions in your interview should be the third unanswered question.

For years, salespeople have been taught that selling means talking, giving a smorgasbord of information about product features and services. There are several problems with this approach to the prospecting portion of the "sales process"—mainly, needs, wants, and problems are different for every prospect. Assuming that your product will be used by each customer for the same purpose in the same way, or to solve similar problems, is one of the most frequent shortcomings of most people selling today. For example, you visit your family physician complaining of stomach pains. Without asking any questions he prescribes a medication to be taken four times a day for thirty days.

Would you follow this advice? I certainly wouldn't. The reason is he doesn't know what's wrong with me unless he probes for information about my problem. I don't really care if he's seen twenty-five patients with stomach problems, every day for ten years. I want him to know my problems.

In my opinion, questions—intelligent, well thought-out, appropriate, and well-timed questions—offer many positive benefits for both the doctor and the salesperson.

First—Questions establish an atmosphere of control. I guarantee, if you turn over your presentation to your prospect, he won't give your presentation as well as you could. If you want to get him talking in a controlled way, I suggest questions are the best way. They put you and keep you in the driver's seat.

Second—Questions help you determine how cooperative your prospect will be. Generally, I have found that prospects who cooperate in the beginning will cooperate throughout the presentation, including the close. Prospects who are difficult or refuse to cooperate in the beginning usually maintain the same stubborn attitude throughout the sales process. The right questions coupled with the right answers help you determine the cooperative nature of the prospect.

Third—Questions get you valuable information about client needs, desires, and problems. Listen. Most prospects are telling you what you need to tell them to sell them, but you have to shut up long enough to hear them.

Fourth—Questions help you identify clients' styles, opinions, their current understanding and awareness of their own needs and your product or service.

Fifth—Questions help you avoid rejection. If, for some reasons (known or unknown) your prospect is not ready to buy from you now, no matter how competent you are, you will leave without a sale. You can increase your closing ratio and reduce your number of rejections through better probing and gain the confidence to terminate when you believe you are not with a quality prospect.

Sixth—Questions build trust and rapport. One of the best compliments you can pay another human being is to be sincerely interested in what he or she has to say. You demonstrate this interest by listening.

Many salespeople are convinced that it is necessary to make several calls to a prospect before you can establish a climate of trust and confidence. Let's use our physician example again. Do you object to his asking you dozens of questions as he completes your patient table with you prior to making a diagnosis and subsequent recommendation? The more he asks you about your condition, the better you feel about his ability to help you and the more confidence you have in him. All he did was ask questions and get you talking, then he listened. And he probably took notes. I suggest you do the same. There is nothing worse than asking questions for fifteen minutes, getting all kinds of valuable information, and then not remembering what was said so you can use the information later in the presentation.

I open all my presentations exactly the same way: I don't know how my company can best serve your needs. The best way for me to determine this is if I can ask you a few questions (or personal questions). Is that okay? Do you mind if I take notes?

Seventh—Questions save you time. If you are unable to get cooperation, advance commitment, or pertinent answers to your questions, you can postpone the presentation to another time when she is a better qualified or more cooperative prospect. Why waste the time in the presentation now? Unless, of course, you don't have anyone else to talk to.

Eighth—Questions keep you from talking too much.

Ninth—Questions get the prospect involved.

Tenth—Questions get and maintain prospect attention.

Eleventh—Questions make your prospect think.

Twelfth—Questions and subsequent answers, if you listen attentively, increase the likelihood that the prospect will listen to you when it is your turn to talk.

Thirteenth—Intelligent questions make you look competent and knowledgeable.

The mind of the prospect must go through four stages psychologically. You must get attention, create interest, cause desire, and get action. In a one-call sales situation you must be able to accomplish all four steps in one presentation. My feeling here is that the moment you feel this prospect is really a suspect, either because his answers are incomplete or wrong (you are unable to generate attention and interest), you should terminate the interview. However, if you are in a multiple-call sale situation (for example, industrial sales, major high-priced products or proposal selling), I believe that no more than four personal calls should be necessary to complete a sale. Why four? No more than one call for each step in the sales process. Attention, one call; interest, one call; desire, one call; action, one call.

Let me present a situation that repeats itself hundreds of thousands of times a day. You see a prospect, give a good presentation, ask for a decision and get a "maybe." Let's stop for a moment and return to the beginning of the sales process. Do you have a suspect or a prospect? What's the difference? A prospect is a prospect and a suspect is a suspect. (I'm not trying to be cute.) What makes a prospect a prospect or a suspect a suspect in your mind is what you know about him or her. You don't change or create prospects or suspects, you discover what they are by gaining information about them. However, before you get any information, you need to know what information you need to determine which they are. Vince Lombardi used to start every football season in the same way, "Gentlemen, this is a football." I believe we need to start at the beginning. First, define what a prospect is for you. Before you begin to ask intelligent questions, you need to know what you need to know.

To help you do this, complete the exercise in Figure 3-A. On the top of the left hand column, write "Information I Need." Complete this side and then prioritize the list. What is the most important thing I need to know? The second most important? And so on.

Question Development

Next, label the top of the right hand column "Question to Ask." Anything that can be misunderstood will be misunderstood. Many salespeople fail to get the information they need simply because they don't ask the right questions or don't ask them in the right way. For each item of information you need, design a question (write it down) so that if you asked it of a total stranger, you would be likely to get the type of answer you wanted.

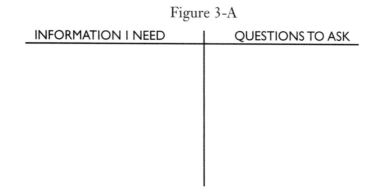

Figure 3-A

INFORMATION I NEED	QUESTIONS TO ASK

After listing the information and questions, prioritize the list on the left in the order of the importance of information needed.

> *Experience keeps a school, yet fools will learn in no other.*
> —Ben Franklin

For example, you are selling real estate and want to know how many children the prospect has and their ages and sex. So, you ask, "Do you have any children?"

"Yes."

"What I meant was, how many children do you have?"

"Three."

"What I meant was, how old are they?"

"12, 16 and 17."

"What sex are they, boys or girls?"

"The oldest two are girls, the youngest, a boy."

That's four questions to get one piece of information. Why not one question, "What are the ages and sexes of your children?" Simple, isn't it? You would be amazed at how much time you waste and how much prospect attention and interest you lose because of poor questions.

Here are some general guidelines in asking questions:

1. Start with broad topics.
2. Keep your questions free of buzz words, jargon, or technical terms.
3. Keep your questions simple; present only one idea at a time.
4. Keep your questions in sequence and in proper focus.
5. Keep them non-threatening and positive.
6. When you must ask a sensitive question, explain why you are asking and indicate the benefits to the prospect for answering.
7. Allow the prospect to answer; don't force an answer.
8. Maintain a consultative atmosphere.
9. Phrase the questions so they are easy to answer.
10. Phrase the questions from the prospect's point of view and psychological level.

General Types of Questions

1. **Open-ended questions:** Cannot be answered with a yes or no, usually begin with how or what, do not lead the prospect in a certain direction, stimulate prospect thinking, increase dialogue.

2. **Closed-ended questions:** Allow specific facts to be developed or uncovered, are simple to answer, are used to solicit feedback, can be used to gain commitment.

3. **Clarifying questions:** Help to get the prospect to further express or elaborate on a point and help to clarify generalizations or misconceptions.

4.   **Leading questions:** Direct the prospect in a predetermined positive direction and give the prospect a way to participate by agreement.

5.   **Assumptive questions:** Check for understanding, predict or cause cooperation and agreement, or disqualification and disagreement.

Develop an example of each.

Learn How to Listen

It is important to know how well you understand and remember what you hear. All of us can profit by listening more closely. A well-trained pair of ears is one of our most valuable assets, and here's why. (See Fig. 3-B)

Experts estimate that most of us spend about 70 percent of our waking hours in some form of verbal communication. It breaks down this way:

Figure 3-B

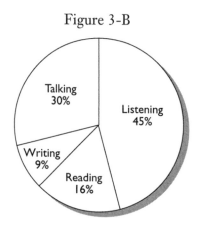

9 percent of our time is spent writing.

16 percent is spent reading.

30 percent is devoted to thinking.

45 percent of the time, almost half the time we are awake, is spent listening.

So you see, it really is a good idea to know how to listen, how to get the most out of what we hear.

Ten Ways to Increase Your Listening Power

Listening power can be increased by:

1. **Recognizing the importance of skillful listening.** If we don't realize it is worthwhile to hear more about what people have to say to us, there is no reason to bother to improve this creative power.
2. **Paying attention.** This may seem too obvious, yet it is surprising how many of us try to fake attention, and it is very embarrassing when we get caught at it. While listening to people, we should look at them. Squarely in the eyes is always best and gives them the attention and respect we appreciate so much when we are speaking. If, instead of listening to a person, we are trying to figure out what we are going to say next, we can't possibly keep up with what that person is telling us.
3. **Keeping alert to the speaker's gestures and facial expressions.** Empathy is one of the outstanding marks of a good listener. None of us likes to talk to someone who persists in wearing a deadpan expression. So try smiling occasionally, or nodding in agreement. This tactic is just as positive as a yawn is negative.
4. **Never rule out any topic of discussion as totally uninteresting.** Creative people are always on the lookout for new and different information. While we might likely classify some topics as drivel (gossip being one candidate for this list), it is wise to be sure the subject is not worthwhile before tuning it out. Keep your mind open to new ideas. They are all around you.
5. **Avoid prejudging the speaker.** Pay attention to what she is saying, rather than the way she is saying it. Close-mindedness and jumping to conclusions might well come under this heading.
6. **Taking brief notes while listening.** When these are reviewed later, they jog the memory and bring back to mind the speaker's dialogue.
7. **Looking for the speaker's purpose, what she is trying to get across.** Search for her main ideas and distinguish fact from fiction.

8. **Being aware of our "emotional deaf spots" that have a tendency to turn off our hearing.** These are often words or ideas that strike us the wrong way. If we know of such "deaf spots," we can begin removing them by defining the word or idea that is bothering us. Analyze the matter completely or discuss it with a good friend or family member. Once we realize that a situation like this exists, it's relatively simple to cure it.

9. **Being observant.** Listen for areas of mutual interest and resist distractions. Our minds can think at speeds of 500 words per minute plus and we normally speak at about 125 words per minute. There are three things we can do to keep our rapid thinking concentrated on what is being said:

    1. Weigh and evaluate the material as we listen. Think more about it.
    2. Think ahead; anticipate the next area to be covered.
    3. Think back. Recapitulate. A quick recap helps our memory; it increases our retention of what we have been told.

10. **Practicing the skills of listening with business associates, friends and family.** By talking about things that are important to us, we reinforce and amplify our own understanding. Good listening pays high dividends in business, in social situations and in our personal lives. A Golden Rule in listening: Always listen to someone the way you would like to be listened to.

The "Maybe"

"I don't know who you are.
I don't know your company.
I don't know your company's product.
I don't know what your company stands for.
I don't know your company's customers.
I don't know your company's record.
I don't know your company's reputation.
Now, what was it you wanted to sell me?"

What we need is not the will to believe, but the wish to find out.
—Bertrand Russell

If you could have your choice would you prefer a "yes," a "no" or a "maybe"?

The curse of the salesperson is the prospect who will not say "yes" and will not say "no," but gives you a "maybe."

Contrary to popular opinion, most prospects do not want to reject you. That is why they say "maybe;" saying "yes" or "no" is too final. Their hope is that with a "maybe" you will slowly drift away and blend into obscurity, relieving them of the need to ever have to give you a "yes" or a "no."

My experience tells me that, through the years, most of the "maybes" I have been given have been postponed "nos." People generally do not like to make decisions and the salesperson who forces a decision is bound to make some prospects uncomfortable.

The other problem with the "maybe" is if you are convinced that this prospect is a serious "maybe," it will take your time and attention to keep the "maybe" alive. If you have too many "maybes" at any one time, you will find you are spending most of your prospecting time keeping the "maybes" alive. As a result you are left with little time to develop other good prospects by other methods.

I don't want, nor will I accept, a "maybe." I would prefer a "no" anytime to a "maybe." At least I know where I stand.

There are exceptions to every rule. Some "maybes" may indeed turn out to be "yeses." But if you are no longer in the business, what good does it do you? The worst human emotion is false hope. And "maybes" are full of false hope. Avoid them at all costs. In most cases they are an excuse. The prospect is not convinced that what you offer will solve his problem or meet his need for the dollars invested. Don't give up—keep selling! "Maybes" can be convinced. They are a challenge and many times this is the point when the pros really begin to sell.

What, up to this point, has been your typical reaction to a "maybe"?

How long and how often must you hear "maybe" before you begin to do something about it? A "no" is better than a "maybe."

People-reading Skills

In this section, we will discuss two approaches to effectively read people's movements, facial expressions, actions, and many other factors that can contribute to your ability to persuade. It has been reported that more than 70 percent of all communication is non-verbal. Many times it's not what prospects say that's important, but how they say it—how they're acting. Prospects can be saying "no" with their eyes, but "yes" with language. Why is this so? And how can we pull together all aspects of communication so that we can tailor our message to a prospect that is both interested and listening?

Behavioral Styles

Some of the information on behavioral styles and body language was taken from the research and work done by Anthony Alesandra in his book, *Non-Manipulative Selling.* *

There are four distinct types of behavioral patterns in people. Generally, we fall into a dominant style and, sometimes, a secondary style. A person can, from time to time, exhibit different behavior from any or all of the four styles, but generally a dominant pattern will emerge.

Before we go on, I would like you to review the charts in Figures 3-C—3-F. Become familiar with each of the four charts and try to determine which style you are. Take ample time to do this. If you don't, the explanations on how to use this excellent selling tool will be useless to you. This information can, when integrated into your selling behavior, substantially increase your efficiency and income.

Non-Manipulative Selling by Anthony J. Alesandra and Philip S. Weller with Jerry D. Dean (Englewood Cliffs, N.J.: Prentice Hall. 1981)

Figure 3-C(a)
BEHAVIORAL CHARACTERISTICS OF EACH STYLE

	Low Assertiveness	High Assertiveness
High Responsiveness	**Amiable Style** Slow at talking action and making decisions. Likes close, personal relationships. Dislikes interpersonal conflict. Supports and actively listens to others. Weak at goal-setting and self direction. Excellent ability to gain support from others. Works slowly and cohesively with others. Seeks security and connectedness. Good counseling skills.	**Expressive Style** Spontaneous actions and decisions. Likes involvement. Dislikes being alone. Exaggerates and generalizes. Dreams and gets others caught up in the dreams. Jumps quickly from one activity to another. Works quickly and excitedly with others. Seeks esteem and connectedness. Good persuasive skills.
Low Responsiveness	**Analytical Style** Cautious actions and decisions. Likes organization and structure. Dislikes involvement. Asks many questions about specific details. Prefers objective, task-oriented environment. Wants to be right—overrelies on data collection. Works slowly and precisely alone. Seeks security and self-actualization. Good problem solving skills.	**Driving Style** Decisive actions and decisions. Likes control. Dislikes inaction. Prefers maximum freedom to manage. Cool, independent, and competitive with others. Low tolerance of attitudes and advice of others. Works quickly and impressively alone. Seeks esteem and self-actualization. Good administrative skills.

Figure 3-C(b)
POSITIVE/NEGATIVE DESCRIPTIONS OF EACH STYLE

	Low Assertiveness	High Assertiveness
High Responsiveness	**Amiable Style** Positive — Negative Supportive — Complying Reliable — Retiring Pleasant — Softhearted	**Expressive Style** Positive — Negative Invigorating — Excitable Optimistic — Impatient Animated — Manipulated
Low Responsiveness	**Analytical Style** Positive — Negative Diligent — Picky Perseverant — Righteous Systematic — Stiff	**Driving Style** Positive — Negative Firm — Uncompromising Comprehensive — Overbearing Productive — Pressuring

Figure 3-D
DOMINANT AND SECONDARY STYLES

	Low Assertiveness	High Assertiveness
High Responsiveness	• Amiable—AMIABLE • Expressive—AMIABLE • Analytic—AMIABLE • Driver—AMIABLE	• Amiable—EXPRESSIVE • Expressive—EXPRESSIVE • Analytic—EXPRESSIVE • Driver—EXPRESSIVE
Low Responsiveness	• Amiable—ANALYTIC • Expressive—ANALYTIC • Analytic—ANALYTIC • Driver—ANALYTIC	• Amiable—DRIVER • Expressive—DRIVER • Analytic—DRIVER • Driver—DRIVER

Figure 3-E
PACE AND PRIORITY STYLES

	Low Assertiveness	High Assertiveness
High Responsiveness	Amiable Style Pace = Slow Priority = Relationships	Expressive Style Pace = Fast Priority = Relationships
Low Responsiveness	Amiable Style Pace = Slow Priority = Tasks	Amiable Style Pace = Fast Priority = Tasks

Figure 3-F

	Low Assertiveness	High Assertiveness
High Responsiveness	Amiable Style Priority-Relationships Pace Problems Slow Pace	Expressive Style Priority-Relationships Priority Problems Fast Pace
Low Responsiveness	Analytical Style Priority-Tasks Priority Problems Slow Pace	Driving Style Priority-Tasks Pace Problems Fast Pace

Pace and Priority Problems of Mixed Styles

Now that you have become familiar with the four types of styles, let's analyze how we can use this information to prospect more effectively.

Let's first look at professions. Where would you expect to find an abundance of **Amiables?** Social work, education, religion? Why not add some to the list?

How about **Expressives?** Sports, the arts, advertising? What else can you think of?

Drivers—Top management, sales, law. Can you add any here?

Analyticals—Science, accounting, engineering. Add some here also.

Dress

The Amiable—soft colors, nothing extravagant or showy. Maybe even a little outdated. Their priority in clothes would be comfort.

The Expressive—lots of color, latest in styles, and high fashion. Might even follow fads.

The Analytical—conservative, last year's fashions, blacks, grays, nothing cheap. Wants a lot of wear from his investment.

The Driver—conservative but current, functional, clothes are important. Clothes that don't get in the way. Some status symbols possibly.

Autos

What kind and color of car would an **Expressive** drive? A Datsun 2802 or TR-6; bright orange, green, yellow.

The Driver—Cadillac, Lincoln, Mercedes; black, white, silver.

The Amiables—four-door sedan, station wagon; light blue, green, tan.

The Analytical—Volvo, Volkswagon, good economy, last a long time, yet functional.

General Appearance

How about personal trappings or facial hair? **The Expressive** could wear a lot of jewelry, the latest hairstyle, a beard.

The Driver—only those items that help get the job done efficiently; calculator, watch, styled hair.

The Amiable—doesn't want to really be noticed or offend anyone.
The Analytical—probably close cropped hair, bun.

What About the Office?

Amiable—Pictures of children, comfortable chairs. They would offer you a cup of coffee.

Analytical—charts, graphs, manuals, calculators. Neat and orderly.

The Expressive—plants, color. Well-decorated, awards.

The Driver—big desk, organized, clutter, functional. "Let's get down to business" attitude. "You're not here to visit."

Stop here. See if you can add any additional descriptive information to each style in each category.

Other areas to look at might be type or style of home, hobbies or outside interests, goals, spouse's behavioral characteristics, selling vocabulary.

Here is an interesting problem. Let's say you, as the salesperson, are a Driver and your prospect is an Amiable. What will be the result? If you guessed conflict, tension, mistrust, you're right! They want small talk. You want to get down to business.

How about the Expressive salesperson with an Analytical prospect? The prospect wants facts, figures, and details. You want to deal in vague generalizations fantastic terms, terrific guarantee, outstanding service. Here again we have conflict, tension, etc. Who should adjust—the salesperson or prospect? I'll bet you said salesperson, but I'll also bet you don't most of the time. You see, you are the style you are. You would rather sell to people like you.

Look over your customer base. I'll wager that most of your customers have styles similar to yours.

Which type of salesperson would you think could be most successful? Amiable (you like people)? No. Driver (let's get the job done)? No. Analytical (I'll flood the prospect with facts, figures, knowledge)? No. Expressive (sell the sizzle only—razzle dazzle them)? No. Who then? I know successful salespeople in all styles. Your success is not what you are, but how well you can adjust your style to the prospect's style.

I also believe you need four completely different sets of behavior and vocabulary to adjust successfully. Study this information and start to look at people as behavioral styles rather than just people. Play with it. It's fun. Use it in your social life, in helping others learn how to motivate themselves and in working with associates. Watch how people respond when you are on their wavelength. I also suggest you read Alesandra's book. Expand your understanding of this excellent method to persuade people by adjusting your own behavior patterns.

Approaching Each Behavioral Style

Each of the four behavioral styles needs to be approached within the framework of that person's style. Your vocabulary, tone, pace, and gestures all should be tailored to his or her particular characteristics. The following four lists can be a starting point in developing these four customer prospect approaches.

Amiable

- Try to support the Amiable's feelings.
- Project that you are interested in your client as a person.
- Take time to effectively get the client to spell out personal objectives. Make sure you get the client to differentiate what he or she wants versus what he or she thinks you want to hear.
- When you disagree with the Amiable, do not debate facts and logic. Discuss personal opinions and feelings.
- If you and the Amiable quickly establish an objective and come to a fast decision, explore potential areas for future misunderstanding or dissatisfaction.
- Be agreeable with the Amiable by casually moving along in an informal, slow manner.
- Show the Amiable you are "actively" listening and you are "open" in your discussions.
- The Amiable guarantees that actions will involve a minimum of risk. Offer personal assurances of support. However, do not overstate your guarantees or you will lose your client's trust.

Analytics

- Try to support the Analytic's organized, thoughtful approach. Any contributions you can make toward the Analytic's objectives should be demonstrated through actions rather than words (send literature, brochures, charts, etc.).
- Be systematic, exact, organized, and prepared with the Analytic.
- List advantages and disadvantages of any plan you propose and have viable alternatives for dealing effectively with disadvantages.
- Give the Analytic time to verify your words and actions (because the client will take the time). The client likes things in writing, so follow-up your personal contacts with a letter.
- Provide solid, tangible, factual evidence (not someone's opinion) that what you say is true and accurate.
- Do not rush the decision-making process.
- An analytic likes guarantees that his or her actions can't backfire.
- Avoid gimmicks which you believe might help you in getting a fast decision (the Analytic will think something is wrong with your plan).

Expressives

- Get your clients to talk about opinions, ideas, and dreams, and then try to support them.
- Don't hurry the discussion. Try to develop mutually stimulating ideas together.
- The Expressive does not like to lose arguments, so try not to argue. Instead, explore alternative solutions you both can share with enthusiasm.
- When you reach an agreement, iron out the specific details concerning what, when, who, and how. Be sure you both agree on the specifics.
- Summarize in writing what you both agreed upon even though it may not appear necessary (don't ask permission, just do it).
- Be entertaining and fast-moving.
- Make sure you both are in full agreement concerning when actions must be performed (specifications).

- The Expressive's decisions are positively affected if you use testimonials from important people or companies with which this client can identify.

Drivers

- Try to support your client's goals and objectives.
- Ask questions that allow a client to discover things rather than be told.
- Keep your relationship businesslike. Do not attempt to establish a personal relationship unless that is one of your client's objectives.
- If you disagree with a Driver, argue the facts, not personal feelings.
- Give recognition to the Driver's ideas, not to the Driver personally.
- To influence the decisions of the Driver, you should provide alternative actions with probabilities of their success (backed by facts, if available).
- Be precise, efficient, time-disciplined and well-organized with the Driver.

Action Types

In addition to behavioral styles, you should be familiar with the following four action personalities. These four types of people exist and should be recognized and then dealt with or sold to, according to their general behavior patterns:

FATALIST

Fear of failure

Everything is futile

Nothing works (futile)

I cant do anything (feeble)

Fabricates

General statement: This person is good only in routine work; they shun responsibility.

How to approach: To sell to this person, you must help him believe in himself and take responsibility for him (if you want to).

EXASPERATOR
Likes to enslave
Energetic
Enforce
Enrage
Likes enmity

General statement: Likes to prove his strength, will argue, even lie, to win or prove a point.

How to approach: Compliment his strengths and performances.

APPRAISER
Absolute
Accurate
Accountable
Anti-social
Actually

General statement: Quiet, perfectionist, lacks emotion, calculating.

How to approach: Give him details, absolutes, and supporting documents and figures.

RELATOR
Ridicule
Respect
Receive
Responsible
Reactionary

General statement: Likes and wants acceptance.

How to approach: Give him approval and appreciation.

Body Language

The concept of body language takes on an entire new meaning, in my opinion, when you blend it with behavioral styles. For example, the prospect who sits with his arms folded: if this were an Analytical, it wouldn't bother me too much. However, if an Amiable did this, caution might be advised. What if a prospect is rigid and inflexible: A driver might normally act this way, but if the Expressive clams up or becomes more passive or rigid, again maybe caution is needed.

Body language by itself only tells part of the story. You must blend it with the psychological level and behavioral style, and then attempt to get a better prospect reading. Having said this, there are a few standard, well-known descriptions of certain types of behavior that you should be familiar with. (See Figure 3-G)

The following is a list of the most popular types of behavior:

1. Openness:
—open hands
—taking coat off
—moving closer
—leaning forward
—uncrossed legs
—arms gently crossing lower body

2. Enthusiasm:
—small upper or inward smile
—erect body stance
—hands open, arms extended
—eyes wide and alert
—lively and bouncy
—voice lively and well-modulated

3. Defensiveness:
—rigid body
—arms/legs crossed tightly
—minimal eye contact
—pursed lips
—head down with chin depressed toward chest
—fists clenched
—fingers clenching crossed arms
—leaning back in chair

4. Angry:
—body rigid
—fists clenched

—lips closed and held in a tight thin line
—continued eye contact with dilation of pupils
—squinting of eyes
—shallow breathing

5. Readiness:
—leaning forward in chair
—hand placed mid-thigh
—relaxed, but alive facially
—standing with hands on hips, feet slightly spread

6. Evaluating:
—slightly tilted head
—sitting front portion of chair with upper torso forward
—hand-to-cheek gesture
—stroking chin or pulling beard

7. Nervousness:
—clearing throat
—hand-to-mouth movements
—covering mouth when speaking
—tugging at ear
—darting eyes
—twitching lips or face
—mouth slightly open
—playing with objects or fidgeting
—shifting weight while standing
—tapping fingers
—waving foot
—pacing
—whistling

8. Suspicion/secrecy:
—failing to make eye contact or resisting your glances
—glancing sideways at you
—rubbing or touching nose
—squinting or peering over glasses

9. Rejection/doubt:
—touching and rubbing nose
—squinting or rubbing eyes

—arms and legs crossed
—body withdrawn
—throat-clearing
—hand-rubbing or ear-tugging
—raising eyebrow

10. Confidence/authority
—steepling—the higher the hands, the greater the confidence
—resting feet on desk
—leaning back with hands laced behind head
—proud erect body stance with chin forward
—continuous eye contact with little blinking

11. Reassurance:
—pinch the fleshy part of hands
—gently rub or caress some personal object—ring, watch
—bite fingernails or examine cuticles

12. Frustration:
—tightly clenched hands or shaking fists
—hand wringing, rubbing back of neck
—controlled short breathing
—blind staring
—running hands through hair
—stamping foot

13. Boredom/indifference:
—head in hand
—drooping eyelids
—relaxed posture, slouching
—tapping foot, fingers
—swinging feet
—blank stares, little eye contact
—doodling
—slack lips

14. Acceptance:
—moving closer to other person
—spreading hands held to chest

One of the best ways to persuade others is with your ears—by listening to them.
—Dean Rusk

Figure 3-G

WHAT ARE THESE PROSPECTS SAYING?

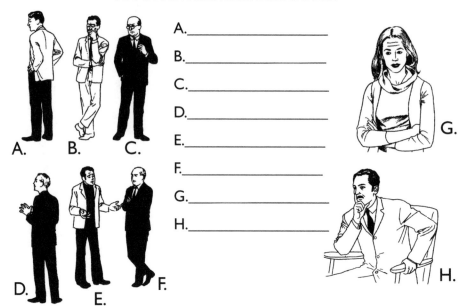

A._____

B._____

C._____

D._____

E._____

F._____

G._____

H._____

Figure 3-H

PROXEMIC ZONES

0–2 feet	intimate
2–4 feet	personal
4–12 feet	social
12 + feet	public

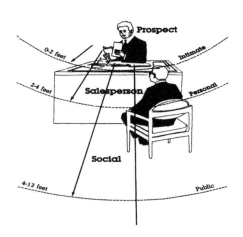

1) Sales relationship should begin in the social zone.
2) Selling should be done in the personal zone.
3) Move closer than four feet only by invitation.
4) If you go into the intimate zone, don't stay there for long periods of time. It makes the prospect nervous.

Neuro-Linguistic Programming (NLP): This information is beyond the scope of this particular book. However, I believe that this concept and others on the horizon will revolutionize how you and I communicate. Keep your mind, eyes, and ears open to new methods and techniques of communications and how to apply them to selling.

Sources of Good Prospects

Prospects and suspects are everywhere. The key is to learn where the best prospects are and how to reach them, and where the worst prospects are and how to avoid them. Rather than give you a lists of sources, as other sales books do, I'd rather give you some clues to use to learn to identify where you can develop an endless supply of highly qualified prospects.

You must first ask yourself a question. Where would you like your customers to come from this year, next year, and as long as you are in sales?

Rather than prospecting, as most salespeople do, taking whomever comes your way, I recommend a more scientific approach. If you could have all your customers coming from one of the following, which would you select?

A. An industry that has peaked and is now on the decline.
B. An industry that is stable, neither growing or slowing.
C. An industry that is getting ready to or is already in an accelerated growth pattern.

If you are like most salespeople, you selected C. Congratulations! But, what are you doing now to see that it happens? For example, what industries really took off during the 1940s? Atomic energy and war industries. Can you think of any others? How about the 50s? Space, pharmaceuticals, television—can you add any to this list? And the 60s. Fast foods, music, recreational travel—think of any more? The 70s—

energy conservation, communications, electronics—what can you add? How would you like to have been Ray Kroc's life insurance salesperson when he started McDonald's? He would have made you wealthy. Enough of history.

Shakespeare said, "There is a tide in the affairs of men which if taken at the flood leads to a fortune."

If only you could see into the future and then position yourself as a supplier to or representative of that industry, your success, would almost be assured. (See Figures 3-I and 3-J)

It is easier to sell people or businesses on the upswing. They are more optimistic about their future, more confident of success and more secure. They buy more and they buy faster. I'm talking about becoming aware of growth trends. It is really quite easy. All you have to do is pay attention to your world. There are some things you can watch, however, that will make the observations easier.

Identifying a Growth-trend Industry

1. A growth industry attracts more young people than old. They want youthful ideas, enthusiasm, and people who aren't saddled with a preconceived "why change" attitude.
2. A growth industry is hungry for lots of people, promotions come fast, expansion is rapid, and the need for people is continuous.
3. Smaller companies in a growth industry are bought or absorbed by larger companies in mergers or acquisitions.
4. Generally the government will finance a growth-trend industry, just as the armed forces financed the development of computers in the 40s and 50s.
5. Growth industries are most often in the news. They are the companies making things happen.

Stop for a few minutes. Relax. What industries are going to take off during the next two decades—and how can you prospect to take advantage of their growth?

I recommend you subscribe to *Omni, Next, Futurist, and Science Digest*, to mention a few. These publications will give you clues as to industry and product trends you can use to prospect more efficiently.

Figure 3-I
MARKET ANALYSIS

1. What is my universe? Where could my business come from? By industry, geographic area, economic level, history:_____

_____

_____

A. What do I need to know about this business?
   Cycle of business_____
   Sales_____
   Who makes the decisions_____
   Number of employees_____
   Is it a good credit risk? What is its rating?_____

2. In what area would I like to operate? Will the travel time cost too much money?
Location:_____ Travel distance:_____ Time:_____ $_____
Location:_____ Travel distance:_____ Time:_____ $_____
Location:_____ Travel distance:_____ Time:_____ $_____

3. What economic areas do I want to deal in? $_____

4. Historically, am I in control of where my business comes from? _____

5. Who are my major competitors?_____

6. What market share are we getting? _____

7. Why are they getting most of the business?
   A. Old established firm _____ B. Good Service _____
   C. Quality product _____ D. Special guarantee_____
   E. Price, are they cheaper? _____ E. Other_____

8. What are my competitors' strong points?_____

_____

9. What are my competitors' weak points? _____

_____

10. Why should my prospects buy my product/service?_____

_____

_____

Figure 3-J
SAMPLE ANNUAL SELLING CURVE

	JAN	FEB	MAR	APR	MAY	JUN	JUL	AUG	SEP	OCT	NOV	DEC
Air conditioner dealers	2.0	2.0	3.9	6.5	13.8	23.0	25.6	12.7	5.4	2.2	1.6	1.3
Appliance stores	6.4	6.3	7.4	7.5	8.3	8.6	8.7	9.0	8.5	8.9	9.3	11.4
Appliance TV repair	7.2	7.0	8.1	8.2	8.6	9.2	8.4	9.0	8.5	9.0	8.6	8.8
Auto dealers (new)	6.3	7.2	9.9	9.5	10.5	9.1	8.5	9.7	8.0	7.2	7.9	6.9
Auto dealers (used)	7.0	7.3	9.2	8.8	9.1	9.1	8.5	8.9	7.7	8.8	8.1	7.5
Auto loans	6.3	7.2	9.6	9.3	9.0	8.9	8.3	9.0	8.5	8.3	8.2	7.2
Auto parts stores	6.9	7.2	9.1	9.2	10.0	8.9	8.6	9.6	8.3	9.2	7.2	6.6
Auto rental	6.7	6.3	8.0	8.4	8.4	9.3	8.5	9.0	8.6	8.1	9.0	9.0
Auto repairs	7.9	7.7	8.8	8.6	8.7	9.0	9.4	8.1	7.9	8.1	7.9	7.5
Bakeries	7.0	7.1	8.4	8.2	8.6	6.5	8.7	9.1	8.6	8.8	8.4	8.0
Banks (savings)	7.2	7.4	8.1	8.2	8.6	8.4	8.2	8.5	8.0	8.9	9.0	9.4
Beauty salons	7.3	7.3	8.5	8.2	8.3	8.7	8.1	8.4	8.6	8.5	8.8	9.4
Bedding stores	6.8	7.5	8.8	7.9	8.7	9.7	7.6	10.4	9.6	9.3	7.4	6.8
Beer	6.8	6.9	9.0	8.8	9.3	20.2	9.3	9.6	8.3	7.9	9.5	7.0
Boating dealers (boats)	6.5	8.3	12.7	12.2	9.8	7.5	6.3	5.9	6.1	6.5	9.3	6.1
Book stores	7.6	6.3	6.9	6.8	7.5	5.1	6.9	9.1	9.5	8.1	9.9	14.6
Bowling lanes	10.1	9.9	10.8	9.7	6.3	12.4	5.1	5.0	8.5	10.0	7.9	9.7
Bridal shops (weddings)	5.3	5.7	6.9	7.5	9.3	9.6	9.3	9.3	8.8	7.9	8.8	8.0
Building supply dealers	5.5	5.5	7.3	7.9	8.8	8.8	9.5	11.0	9.5	10.0	8.3	7.4
Camera stores	7.3	7.1	8.0	7.8	8.4	8.3	8.2	10.2	8.0	8.8	9.2	11.5
Carpet stores	6.8	6.7	8.4	8.5	8.7	5.5	8.2	8.7	8.5	8.8	9.2	8.8
Catalog showrooms	4.6	4.2	4.4	4.7	6.2	8.0	4.6	4.9	6.2	8.7	16.3	29.7
Children's wear stores	4.0	5.0	9.0	6.0	7.0	8.0	6.0	9.1	11.0	9.0	11.0	14.0
Clock shops	5.0	6.0	7.0	6.0	6.0	8.0	9.0	10.0	12.0	11.0	11.0	9.0
Confectionary stores	7.8	9.0	8.7	7.2	6.8	6.3	5.4	10.0	10.5	10.3	9.6	8.8
Credit cards	7.5	6.4	7.5	7.6	8.3	8.4	8.1	9.8	8.7	8.8	9.1	10.5
Dairies	8.1	7.4	8.2	8.3	8.5	8.1	8.5	9.2	8.6	8.7	8.5	5.6
Department stores (total)	5.4	5.5	7.3	7.6	7.9	7.9	7.5	8.5	8.0	8.5	10.2	16.0
Department stores (chain)	5.8	5.8	7.5	7.7	8.4	8.1	7.7	8.2	7.6	8.0	9.7	15.1
Discount stores	5.5	5.2	7.6	6.8	7.5	9.1	7.2	8.6	8.8	8.4	10.0	15.9
Drug stores	7.5	7.4	8.1	7.9	8.2	8.1	8.0	8.0	8.0	8.3	8.4	11.8
Electric utilities (residential)	9.7	9.6	8.5	7.4	6.9	7.5	8.1	8.3	8.8	7.7	7.4	8.5
Farm equipment	6.0	4.8	8.0	10.4	8.3	10.8	8.7	9.3	9.9	14.7	4.9	6.1
Fast food	7.0	6.9	8.2	8.3	9.0	9.3	9.6	7.4	8.3	8.1	7.7	8.2
Finance companies	6.1	6.7	8.0	8.6	9.4	8.5	9.1	9.2	7.8	9.4	8.5	8.8
Formal wear stores	4.7	5.8	6.0	7.9	16.7	11.4	7.0	9.9	6.7	5.7	7.2	10.9
Funeral homes	9.4	8.3	8.6	8.2	7.9	7.9	8.2	7.7	7.7	8.4	8.2	8.9
Furniture stores	6.9	6.9	8.0	7.9	8.3	8.5	8.6	9.1	8.3	8.6	9.2	9.7
Gasoline stations	7.3	7.0	7.8	8.0	8.4	8.6	8.8	9.0	8.6	8.8	8.7	9.0
Hardware stores	5.7	5.5	7.4	8.4	9.3	9.3	8.7	8.8	8.7	9.1	8.9	10.3
Hi-fi stereo	7.3	7.1	7.9	7.1	7.3	8.0	8.0	8.3	8.4	8.4	9.1	13.2

HOW TO READ THIS CHART: The percent under every month is the percent of yearly sales all retailers do that month. Source: Radio Advertising Bureau

It is the individual who knows how little he knows about himself who stands
a reasonable chance of finding out something about himself before he dies.
—S. I. Hayakawa

Prospect Profile

Using a prospect profile in your prospecting can offer you two important advantages:

First, it can show you potential prospecting danger areas.

Second, it can point out obvious ways you can improve your income and results through a smarter, more effective approach to the entire area of new customer development.

What is a prospect profile? Let's say that your average client is 45 years old, female and a business owner for at least five years.

George, a good friend, gives you a referral. The person is 39 years old, a man, and executive vice president of a small manufacturing company.

The same day, Joann also a friend gives you another referral to Pam, who is forty-three years old, owns her own gift shop and has had the business for four and a half years.

Who, based on your typical customer profile (from your average profile) is your better prospect?

Obviously, Pam would be the person you would contact first. She is a better match to your typical customer profile. How do you develop this customer profile?

Review your client customer base. Look for key areas that are important to you either by their spending potential, need for your product of service, growth potential, income or sales bracket, or any other area that you believe represents a good customer for you.

Now, whenever you get a referral just compare it to your typical profile. You can make your prospect contact decisions a little more scientifically.

Of course, this system works best when you consistently have more prospects than you can ever see.

I mentioned earlier that using this system can be both positive or negative.

First, the Positive

Let's say you are now earning $30,000 a year and your average customer is a business that buys an average month's advertising of $1,000 from you.

During the next year, you want to increase your income to $60,000. You have three ways to go—double your number of customers, double the amount your average customer spends or combine improvements in both areas to accomplish your goal.

The Negative

Your income is $18,000 a year—your average client is a newlywed couple. You are comfortable calling on this type of prospect and you continue to sell them because they are easy for you to talk to, or relate to, you are comfortable there. However, you have a goal to earn $36,000 this year.

Your choice may be to sacrifice the additional $18,000 in income or sacrifice that comfortable feeling of calling on this kind of prospect.

Methods of Prospecting

Referrals: Most salespeople admit they would like to have more referred leads, but they just don't seem to get their share. I would like to give you my ten step program to more and better referrals. If you follow these guidelines, you will be able to do better than 90 percent of your new business from referrals. It can work for you if you will work at it.

Step one: What is a referral? It is only a name until you have the right to use the leverage of the person giving the name by using his name, and you have qualified the prospect in the same way you would any other name.

Many people think they have referrals when the customer says something like, "I'll give you the name, but don't say I sent you." Without the third-party credibility you may as well go to the white pages of the telephone book, open to any page, and start calling.

A referral should be a qualified name, given to you by a person that either has leverage or credibility with the person being referred. In addition, the person providing the referral will be willing to make a contact for you in some way, or will allow you to use his or her name.

Step two: Why would you want to work with more referrals? Many times, a person giving you a referral will do some selling for you. I have found through the years that most people will believe what someone they know says about you or your product or service more than they will believe what you say about yourself or your own product.

Fear is an important emotion that can get in the way of many sales. One way to quiet the prospect's fear is to be recommended by someone he knows or respects. Your job is to build a referral base that constantly keeps your prospect pipeline full. The most effective way to prospect from referrals is to constantly get 50 percent more prospects than you need. The process is then one of always working with the cream, leaving the milk behind. Every time you receive new referrals, you rate them against the existing file. Many of your current qualified referrals may be shoved aside temporarily or even permanently by a continuous flow of even higher-caliber referrals.

Step three: If you want them, why don't you have more referrals? I've asked this question of thousands of salespeople. One answer comes up 95 percent of the time: "I don't ask." For some strange reason, you expect your customers, friends and acquaintances to automatically send you well-qualified referrals. Your system obviously isn't working because they aren't.

Why don't you ask? Well, one reason is that friendly old devil, "Fear of Rejection." "I want you to like me and I don't want you to refuse to give me names." So how do you avoid the rejection? You don't ask. In reality, your customer wants to give you referrals—and he wants you to sell them. That not only makes him look good, but is also says, "I guess I did a smart thing after all. See, others I know or respect are also buying." Getting referrals should be an automatic part of every sales presentation and social or business contact. You should develop a daily "referral awareness." The second reason you don't ask is because you don't know how to ask.

Step four: Where can you get more referrals? I could answer this question in one word. But it would make the book shorter and you wouldn't feel like you were getting your money's worth. Where? From customers—friends, suppliers, and non-competing salespeople, to mention a few. For example, what does the salesperson who sells $500 suits

have in common with the person who sells Cadillacs? Yes, the same cal-
iber prospect. But their products don't compete. Why not get to know
salespeople in your market who share your prospects? Interesting
thought, isn't it? Why not start a monthly swap club of some kind? How
about your suppliers? They know you and your product or service. Why
not join a business organization and begin to cultivate people who can
give you referrals? Well, I've done enough thinking for you. Have you
got any ideas? (Referrals can come from everywhere!)

Step five: How do you ask for them? Years ago, I developed a technique for getting referrals that I have used ever since. It can work no matter what you sell. Here are the words and the reasoning behind the words:
"Mr. Smith, I have found that all successful people have one thing in common and I'm sure you're no different." (You have accused Mr. Smith of
being successful, but very indirectly. Don't worry, he won't mind the compliment and it's also unlikely that he will know what you are doing.) "You
see, I have found that all successful people like to see other people grow,
improve, and also become more successful." (You're setting him up psychologically, but he loves it. And, by the way, it's true. Successful people do
like to help other people become more successful.) Stop reading for just a
minute. Ask yourself, "How many people do I know?" I mean relatives,
friends, associates—200, 500, 1,000? Would you agree that most people
know at least 200 people? But when you ask people whom do they know
who would be interested in your product or service, what do most of them
say? "I don't know anyone." They do. But they don't want to have to go
through the mental effort to think who would and who wouldn't be interested. Let's put a twist into it. "Mr. Smith, who do you know that owns his
own business? Lives next door? Was just promoted? Moved into the area?"

You ask the question of Mr. Smith, in such a way that the answer to
the question is a name. You help him focus on a specific area in his group
of 200 people. Make it easy for him to help you. Repeat this process
until you get several names. You can get as many names as you want. You
should set the limit, not the person giving the names.

How do you arrive at which types of prospects to ask for? Where do you
want your customers to come from next year and so on? If you want to specialize in contractors, you would ask, "Mr. Smith, whom do you know in the
contracting business?" How about the growth industries we just discussed?

Step six: The next step is to qualify the referrals. Let's assume Mr. Smith has given three names, Bob F., Jim R., and Joan P. Do you know these people? No, who does? He does, and he is in the position to qualify them for you. So let him do it. Here's how. "Mr. Smith, if you were me, which one of these people would you contact first?" (The purpose of this question is to help him prioritize the three for you in his mind.) Mr. Smith says, "Well, I believe I would call Joan P. first." He must have chosen her first for a reason. Let's find out what that reason is. "That's an interesting choice. Why did you select her first?" (Now he will qualify her for you and give you key information which could help you sell her.)

What if Mr. Smith does not volunteer enough of the right information? Be prepared to ask further qualifying questions. What is her position? How long have you known her? Here is where you get the details to plug into your prospect profile. Having received information about Joan P., would you then qualify the other names at this time in this much detail? I wouldn't. "Mr. Smith, permit me to get back to you in the next few weeks with further information on Jim and Bob."

Step seven: Next, there are two ways you can continue. Ask Mr. Smith to call her now and set up an appointment for you, or ask him this question, "Mr. Smith, would you have any objections to picking up the phone in the next few days and calling Joan and mentioning my name and product?" (Would he agree to do this if he had intentions of saying anything bad about you? If so, why is he calling? It only makes him look bad. Remember, he bought. That's the very reason he will do a lot of your selling for you. You are capitalizing on his enthusiasm for you, your product and his pride on his recent purchase.)

Step eight: You then pick up the phone in a day or so and ask Joan, "Did Mr. Smith recently call you and mention my name?" If he did, use the leverage and immediately go for me sale or appointment. You can assume she is between the attention and interest stage. If Mr. Smith hasn't called, your mentioning his name and implying that Mr. Smith was to call will create curiosity—thus attention and interest are again created. At this point, use your telephone approach for referrals. (If you don't have one, we'll cover that in the next section). Later in the week or month, call Mr. Smith back and mention that you are getting ready to call Bob F. "What can you tell me about him?"

Another way to use this step is to ask Mr. Smith to write a short introduction for Joan or Bob on his business card. For example, "Mr. Smith, would you have any objections to writing Joan a short note of introduction for me?" When he agrees, then ask him to take out his business card, turn it over and write the following:

"Joan, this is to introduce Tim Connor. He has some great ideas about saving money, increasing sales, improving productivity"—whatever your product does. "Please give him the courtesy of a few minutes—signed, Mr. Smith." Now you can mail this card with a note and follow it up with a telephone call or drop by in person and hand Joan or Bob the card.

What if the person refuses to let you use his name when you contact the person referred? First of all, if you can't sell him on the use of his name, don't accept the names. "Obviously, Mr. Smith, there is some reason in the back of your mind why you don't want me to use your name. Do you mind if I ask what it is?" (Then deal with it as a standard objection—Chapter 5.) Usually he is afraid his relationship with the person being referred will be hurt by your calling on him. He is looking for reassurance. "Mr. Smith, do you feel I presented myself and my product in a professional manner? Is there any reason to believe that I would approach Joan any less professionally? You may recall that Mr. Jones recommended you to me. Are you glad now that he did? Do you have any objections now if I use your name?"

Step nine: When should you ask for referrals? Immediately after you have closed the sale and before you ask for a deposit or payment. You must make him think it is a part of your presentation and when you ask for money, psychologically, he'll think you are finished. This is the moment that he is most sold on you and your product. After you qualify the referral, thank him and tell him you will let him know how you make out.

Step ten: There is one additional important point in the referral system process. You must report back to Mr. Smith and let him know how you did with his referral—whether it was positive or negative. If it was positive, ask for another referral to replace the one you sold. The more he gives you and the more you sell, the more you will begin to develop a referral base where people are combing the marketplace for you. (Some salespeople call these people bird dogs, implying that you pay for the lead.) They do it because it makes them feel good, and they help people by introducing them to you and your product. If the result was negative, explain why—that it wasn't the product, but the prospect's current status—and ask for another referral. (See Figure 3-K)

A different psychology comes into play here. On the first referral you weren't successful—and he wants you to succeed—so he will try harder to give you a better referral the second time. Just because you had a negative result, don't stop. Give him a chance. Explain the type of prospect you are looking for. Educate him a little on the type of person you want to see. He will cooperate if you let him.

Figure 3-K

CLIENT REFERRAL RECORD

Name_____ Co._____

Address_____

Bus. Phone_____Home Phone_____

Date	Referral Given	Action Taken	Follow Up

Centers of Influence

How would you like to get two or three calls a month that go something like this? "Hello, Tim. This is Jan. I met a man last week that I believe is a good prospect for you. He is a client (friend, employee, etc.) of mine. I told him all about you and your product. He is interested and would like you to call him. By the way, he has the money and the ability to make a buying decision. Good luck!" This person could be considered a center of influence. A center of influence is someone who is interested in your success, believes in your product or service, has influence over a group of people who could be prospects for you and will help you qualify them. How and where do you find such people? If you only had a few you would be guaranteed several sales a month, because centers don't send you prospects or suspects. They send you customers.

More men are killed by overwork than the importance of the world justifies.
—Rudyard Kipling

The center of influence method is relatively easy. First, find them. Second, learn about them, their interests, hobbies, needs, or desires. Then decide how you can help them in any of those areas. Third, educate them and build a psychological debt. What is a psychological debt? The best example I can give you is the following: You have just completed a good sales presentation. You have stroked the prospect, educated the prospect, helped him, and invested time in him. He owes you. How does he pay you? "Boy, Tim, you're a great salesperson." You see, psychologically you have built up a debt. He wants the scale even, so he must repay you. By complimenting you, and your accepting the compliment, the debt is paid. But you can' take compliments to the bank. My experience has been that the compliment was usually in place of an order. But you want orders.

So stop accepting the compliments. I know it doesn't make any sense, but the next time someone says you are a great salesperson and you know it's their payoff for not buying, just say, "I'm sorry, but I just can't accept the compliment." The debt still exists. Watch them, they will go to great lengths to even the debt. Your only acceptable payment is an order.

The way you can build this same kind of debt to be used profitably is to do something of value or provide your center of influence with ideas of information that may not even be related to your product or service. Develop the interest in helping them and they will do likewise. But you must make the first move. First, you do your part. You must earn their willingness to help you. Centers are money in the bank. When properly educated and developed, they can greatly assist your selling career. Don't underestimate their potential. (See Figure 3-L)

Figure 3-L

CENTER OF INFLUENCE RECORD

Name_____ Co._____

Address_____

Bus. Phone_____Home Phone_____

Position_____Secretary/Personal Asst._____

Personal Interests_____

Business Interests_____

Date	Referral Given	Action Taken	Follow Up

Developing Present Customers

Your present customer base can be your best source of new business. Or you can take the attitude, "I'll take the money and run." Many salespeople today would rather cultivate new ground on a regular basis than to return to the original soil and cultivate it for maximum results. I think you are making a big mistake if a large percentage of your new business is not coming from your current customers.

This business can come in one of four ways. First, if you prospected in a growth industry you will grow as your customer grows. As he or his company becomes more successful, you can take advantage of that growth. If you are taking this approach with enough customers, then your natural growth can be plotted exactly along the same scale as your customers. Second, it's more rewarding and satisfying to see a customer grow through the use of your product than to always be testing new markets or prospects. Third, you build a reputation through service, which is the best way to grow and prosper. Your customers will talk about you, prospect for you and become full-time ambassadors. This takes time and commitment, but it's worth it. Fourth, your current customers, when properly developed, will provide you with an endless flow of referrals.

Group Prospecting

Group prospecting is by far the most profitable and rewarding method of cultivating new business for several reasons:

1. You save time. If you can get yourself in front of fifteen people at one time rather than one, you can see more people during your selling day.
2. Because you increase your flow of prospects by the group rather than one at a time, your prospect file tends to remain full.
3. You can successfully weed out obvious suspects.
4. You develop a higher degree of awareness for you and your product.
5. Generally, only the most successful salespeople prospect through groups—so the competition is not as stiff. Yes, you'll be competing with the best, but they will make you better faster than competing with the average producers in your industry.
6. It's fun. Try giving a group presentation once. When you leave with several sales instead of one, you'll enjoy your profession more each day.

How do you prospect for groups? Ask yourself—"Where do my prospects gather, in groups? What meetings do they attend? What clubs, associations, or organizations do they belong to?" (Once you have identified sources, then develop a short presentation designed to entertain, educate and convince your prospects you are a credible force in your industry, a person who would be good for them to know or work with and buy from.) Right now you have some valuable information that some group would be interested in—information that would make their lives easier, more productive, secure, successful, etc. Design a short speech that provides them with that information. As you give the talk you create credibility for yourself, and the right to present your product or service at the end of the talk. Generally, people will be more favorably disposed toward you if you don't mix the talk with the commercial.

Radiation

When you throw a pebble into a quiet pool of water, it sends out from the center a ripple effect of concentric circles. Think of yourself at the center. You can prospect out in any direction. You can literally prospect around every point of the compass. However, some points might be more profitable than others. Radiation in prospecting is where you select or carve out a piece of the total circle, like a piece of pie, and concentrate or specialize.

For example, let's assume you sell only to restaurant owners, dentists, newlyweds, etc. You concentrate in fully developing that market to its potential. You become the expert for your product in that market. When you completely saturate your market or territory, you can branch out or select another piece of the pie.

You can also work on more than one area at a time. There are two real advantages to prospecting in this manner:

First—You will find that people in similar businesses or business situations talk to each other a great deal about ideas, suppliers, and experiences. You can become well-known (but not overnight) in your market area as the person to contact for your type of product or service.

Second—By specializing in an industry or special group through increased activity in that area, your knowledge of the industry's problems and needs increase. You can then use this knowledge to better sell new prospects in the same field. Your knowledge of their needs and problems will give you increased credibility with your prospect. I believe there are many industries that, depending on your product or service, can save you a tremendous amount of time and improve your selling efficiency if prospected in this way. Ask yourself, what would be a good industry to specialize in because of your age, position, sex, color, personal interests, background, or any other special criterion?

Testimonials

Many times in the sales process the prospect asks himself, "Can I trust this person? Can I believe what he is saying? Is he telling me the whole truth?" These questions in the prospect's mind can cause buyer fears that can stand in the way of a successful sale. The fears should be anticipated and solutions to them prepared. They should be quieted before they become a problem and kill an otherwise good sales approach and presentation.

Third-party testimonials are an excellent way to quiet these fears. Many times a person will believe what a total stranger will say about you even though they won't believe what you say about yourself or your own product.

There are several types of testimonials:

First—A third-party introduction by a telephone call or written letter, note or business card.

Second—A photograph of you with your customer and the product or service showing his acceptance and happiness.

Third—A recorded message on a cassette tape—similar to a radio or TV testimonial commercial.

Fourth—A letter of testimony written on the customer's letterhead. This type, in my opinion, is the best—if the letter follows these guidelines: Ask your customer to answer the following four questions in writing and you will have a letter of testimony that is powerful, persuasive, and will get the job done for you.

1. Why did you do business with me, or my firm, or with my product or service?

2. Specifically, what benefits did you gain? Or how did I help you? Or what did we do for you?

3.   Would you recommend me or my company or my product to other individuals or companies?

4.   May I have anyone call you to verify the truth of this letter? Very few people ever call, but you don't want your customer bombarded with calls—or do you? People love to give advice and asked their opinions. I've had clients call me and tell me who called them and what was said. If you are going to use a letter of testimony from a client, make sure you are servicing the client well (that is, if you want a favorable report).

When I get letters of testimony, I always underline the key ideas or phrases. Most people don't take time to read the whole letter. Your eyes immediately focus on the underlined words and sentences. I would not show a prospect more than three or four letters no matter how many you have, and I don't show letters from a customer in one industry to a prospect in the same industry. You might wonder why! I don't want the prospect to really know the customer giving the letter. There is always a tendency to prejudge. "The XYZ Company needed…I know its problems…It isn't that successful…We're not in that same position."

Cold Calling

The traveling salesperson was anxious to gain admission to the office of a prominent industrialist. Establishing business relations with him would be the highlight of the salesperson's whole trip. But the man in question was difficult to see. Entering his outer office, the salesperson gave his card to the secretary. It was taken within and, through the partly opened door, the salesperson saw the executive tear it in half and throw it into the wastebasket. The secretary returned meanwhile and stated that her employer would not see him. "May I have my card back?" asked the salesperson. Slightly embarrassed, the secretary reported to her boss, who sent her back to the outer office with a nickel and a message that he was sorry, but the card had been destroyed. More than equal to the occasion, the salesman drew another card from his wallet and gave it to the woman. "Take this back to him," he said, "and tell him I sell two cards for a nickel." He got his interview and an order.

Those of you who make your living cold-calling and spend a great deal of your prospecting time in this way are wasting valuable time.

At $1.50 for a gallon of gas and $50 per pair for new shoe leather, the cost-return ratio is too low for me. During the '60s, I made an excellent income from primarily a cold-calling system. But times have changed; during the next ten or twenty years, the cold-calling salesperson will become nearly extinct in my opinion.

Why do I feel this way?

1. Mail orders will increase during the next decade.
2. New forms of communication devices will enable the buying public to purchase more easily by computer and telephone. You can't afford to spend your limited amount of time and capital using this slipshod, hit-or-miss prospecting approach. Once in a while, maybe, but not on a regular basis.

For those of you who would like an approach to the cold call, let me share the two methods I have used.

Planned cold-calling: If you must cold-call, I suggest a planned approach. In the planned method you know where you are going, who you want to see, and what you expect to say or sell. But you have no appointment. Here are two openings that, in my opinion, will go a long way in streamlining your cold-call activity.

First—"Good morning, Mr. Jones. My name is Tim Connor. I didn't stop by today to take your valuable time to try to sell you (whatever). I only stopped to ask you a couple of quick questions to determine if my idea for (saving money, increasing sales, improving efficiency, productivity—insert whatever your product or service will do) will be of interest to you. May I ask you just two questions?"

Are you interested, as many (accountants, business owners—substitute his category or profession) are in (saving money, time, etc.)? If I had an idea that you believed would help you (repeat save money, increase sales, etc.), would you be open-minded enough to take a look at it? What would be more convenient for you, to do it now, or next week?" (Either go for the appointment now or for a future appointment.)

Second—"Good morning, Miss James. My name is Tim Connor. I don't have an appointment, but I would like the opportunity to talk with Ms. Smith. I'm sure she, like other successful people (executives) is busy. I didn't stop today to see her, but to set up an appointment with her. Will you please ring her office and announce me?" This whole sequence completely disarms most of her standard answers or objections, unplanned. However physical cold-calling is a waste of valuable time, energy, and money.

Direct Mail

I don't like direct mail as a sales tool. Direct mail is good for exposure and awareness, but unless you are in the mail-order business, direct mail is a crutch that will take up valuable time and give you a false sense of security. Use direct mail to keep your name in front of your best prospects and customers and those customers that you see frequently. But, don't rely on it to sell your product. Before I send out literature to a prospect, I qualify him or her thoroughly on the telephone. If I'm convinced he or she is a prospect, I will send out a limited amount of literature. But I prefer to deliver it. The potential for business is also a consideration here. Chasing small prospects leaves little time for the bigger ones.

Pre-approach Mail

Pre-approach mail differs from direct mail in several ways:

First—Pre-approach is more of a targeted type of mail prospecting where you send out fewer letters, but each has a specific purpose aimed at a specific prospect.

Second—In pre-approach mail, you close the letter stating that you will take some action; e.g., follow-up with a telephone call or stop by.

Third—Pre-approach mail sent out on a regular basis should be followed up no later than two or three days after the prospect receives it. Sending out mail of this type also forces you into a minimum amount of prospecting activity each week.

Pre-approach mail must take the mind of the prospect through the same four steps as in prospecting. A good letter gets attention first, then creates interest (describe a major benefit that your product offers), causes desire (by appealing to dominant emotional buying motive, see

Chapter 5), and produces action (closes with an appeal for an appointment, decision, or some other type of prospect action).

Following are some sample pre-approach letters.

Attention   Dear Mr. Smith,

I'd like to make an exchange with you. For twelve minutes of your time, I'll give you 208 extra hours this year. That sounds exaggerated, but I think it is true. My firm has spent many years developing a new, dry, high-speed office copier. Test after test, under customer use, has shown that the average time an executive saves by putting the machine on his desk is four hours a week...208 hours a year.

Interest   When I see you, I won't have much to say. Our machine, the E-Z Office Copier, will do most of the talking. All I ask is the opportunity to put it on your desk, give you one brief demonstration, and then let you use it yourself so that you can fully appreciate the ease and speed of operation and the quality of the sharp, clean, dry copies it produces.

Action   For myself, I'll reserve the pleasure of telling you how low the investment is. I plan to call you on Tuesday morning to request the courtesy of fifteen minutes.

Sincerely,

Attention   Dear Mr. Jones,

My career is dedicated to shocking people. There are two things I've observed. One is that the Research Division of the Social Security Board has learned that 70 percent of family heads over the age of sixty-five have less than $2,000 when they retire. That certainly is shocking. The second observation is that most people are deeply involved in the daily business of making enough income to handle today's high prices and high taxes.

Interest   They seldom take time out to look ahead and to make plans that may spare them from being part of that shockingly large group. To hear my ideas and suggestions will cost you nothing and will create no obligation. I'm confident you will find our meeting will give you some useful ideas, whether or not you adopt any specific proposals I may make.

Action   I plan to call you next week to determine your interest in this idea.

Sincerely,

Attention   Dear Ms. Lamb,

No one ever spends money through me. That's a peculiar statement from a salesperson, but it happens to be true. My role is to help people review their financial situations and their future needs. If, through my years of training and experience in helping many clients, I see opportunities for financial improvement, I point them out. If they accept my suggestions, they don't spend

Interest   money; they transfer money from one place to another …but only if they are convinced that they may be better off by doing so.

Whether or not I can prove helpful to you remains to be seen. Perhaps you'll agree, though, that you owe yourself the opportunity to find out. There's no fee for counseling and you are under no obligation to accept any ideas I may propose. I plan to call you on Thursday evening to request the courtesy of an appointment.

Sincerely,

Effective Telephone Use

In this section, I will offer you some standard telephone guidelines to which I have added a twist to make them more effective. If they don't work for you as presented, improve them with your own twist.

For referrals: "Good morning, Mrs. Edwards. My name is Tim Connor. Do you have a minute to chat? Mr. Smith, whom I met with last week suggested you were the type of person who is always looking for new ideas to (increase sales, improve personal security, save time, whatever your product or service does). May I ask you a couple of quick questions? Are you interested in (increasing sales, reducing overhead, etc.)? If you believed I had an idea that would help you (save time, make money, etc.) would you be open-minded enough to share a few minutes with me discussing this idea? If you believed strongly that this idea could (save time, etc.) would anyone else need to be present to make a decision?

What would be a good day for you next week, Tuesday or Wednesday? 10:00 .in the morning or 3:00 in the afternoon? Fine. I'm putting that in my calendar. Would you please give me directions to your office? Thank you. I'm looking forward to meeting with you! Goodbye."

This same process can be used in cold telephone calls by only changing the opening. It would go something like this: "Good morning. Mr. Jones. My name is Tim Connor with School for Salespeople. Do you have a minute to chat? The purpose of my call is to determine if I have an idea you believe can help you (save time, make money, etc.). May I ask you just a few quick questions?" and so on.

Pre-approach Telephone Call

In the pre-approach letter you should have closed with: "I plan to call you on Tuesday, next week, etc., to request the courtesy of a brief appointment." When you call as a follow-up to this letter: "Good morning, Mr. Jones. This is Tim Connor. Did you receive the letter I recently sent you?" If he says "yes," assume a close and immediately ask for the appointment. It isn't necessary to repeat everything in the letter. If he says he didn't get it, turn to either the cold-call telephone approach or the referral telephone approach—whichever applies.

General Telephone Guidelines

1. Use a mirror—write "smile" on it. Be happy.
2. Watch your voice and diction—enunciate clearly—speak into telephone softly, use inflection in your voice and raise it at the end of sentences.
3. Set telephone goals—for calls, presentations, closes.
4. Keep telephone records for calls, presentation, appointments.
5. Set aside a certain time each day of the week for telephoning.
6. Be prepared—have prospect cards, pen, calendar, etc., handy.
7. Start with a winning attitude. Expect to be enthusiastically received.
8. Decide what it is you're going to say (telephone presentation).
9. Lighten the mood by making fun of yourself (first thirty seconds).
10. Practice. Use a tape recorder.
11. Never have people call back. (You lose control. They may call back when you're not ready.)
12. Ask questions and listen.
13. Get the prospect talking. Get him involved.
14. Work only by appointments. It shows you value your prospect's time. (Your time is also valuable.)
15. Make appointments a week in advance (at least). If you can see someone tomorrow, it shows them you aren't too busy and probably aren't too successful.
16. Call and confirm appointments the day you have them.
17. If you have secretarial assistance, send out a written confirmation.
18. Be FRIENDLY, SINCERE, ENTHUSIASTIC!
19. Determine the behavioral style and communicate in his style.
20. Take notes.

Some Common Do's and Don'ts

Do's
- Use short, simple, uncomplicated words.
- Use the present tense as much as possible.
- Use words that create a mental image.
- Use words that the listener doesn't have to translate.
- Use words that appeal to the senses and basic psychological needs.
- Pace your voice to the prospect's voice speed.

Don'ts
- Don't use general, complicated, technical words.
- Don't overuse certain words.
- Don't overuse I-me-my.
- Don't use words with ambiguous meanings or buzz words.
- Don't use slang, colloquialisms, foreign words, or jargon.

Getting Advance Commitment

If you could determine in the beginning of the interview whether your prospect was going to buy from you, rather than finding out at the end, as most sales people do, you could save yourself a great deal of time and unnecessary rejection. But how? It's a device I call closing on advance commitment. It's like a game of "let's pretend." In other words, you are saying to the prospect up front: "If I can, will you?" If he will play, you can close the sale in the first ten to fifteen minutes. It goes something like this. After you have completed your initial phase of opening questions and information gathering, and you believe you have identified the real need or problem, you then go into the advance commitment dialogue.

Getting to Decision Makers

It takes one level of understanding to buy a product or service and another level to sell a product or service. Don't let anyone ever convince you that they will discuss your proposal or presentation with their spouse, partner, executive committee, or whatever. I'll bet if they do, they won't do half the job you could have—for two reasons first. They won't have the understanding you do and will therefore attempt to sell logically. People don't buy logically. Second, their retention is short. If their attempt to sell for you is several hours or days after your presentation, they will remember little of what was discussed and will have to rely on printed literature or written proposals. Either way, you lose an important element of the sales process—control!

Getting to decision makers is easy if there is a problem or need that is evident and you have the courage to ask and stand your ground. Let's talk about that. It has been my experience that when a middle person will not allow me to present my product or service to the decision maker, it is for one of three reasons:

First—Fear. The middle person does not know how the decision maker will react to you or your idea. If the decision maker accepts you or the product, the middle person looks good. If, however, the decision maker does not buy or accept the idea, for whatever reason, the middle person feels threatened. If top management does not encourage risk taking and creativity, this type of middle person will fight with determination to keep you out. He or she would rather do nothing than be wrong and cause top management to look down disapprovingly. Again, the motivation for this middle person is the fear of rejection. So, he is not rejecting you; rather, he is protecting himself.

Second—Insecurity. The middle person with any degree of personal or business insecurity will not permit you to go over his head. Your presence threatens his position. For example, consider the sales manager who will not use outside training. He believes the outside person undermines his credibility. The contrary is true. Usually, when an outsider comes in and advises, he reinforces many of the existing methods and policies. It's like parents who try to shelter their children from the outside world. Sooner or later children discover this world for themselves, and this does more to hinder credibility than if the children could have had the information early and from the best source—the parent.

Third—A lack of understanding or awareness of the need or problem. If the middle person does not have full understanding of the immediacy of the need or problem, his tactic may be to procrastinate. He may also feel inadequate because you seem to have a better understanding of the problem than he does.

All of these reasons threaten the security, recognition, or self-esteem of the middle person depending on which psychological level he or she is in.

The best approach is to let him know you understand and empathize with his position, but that nothing you do will in any way make his life more complicated or difficult. What he really needs is reassurance. You must also be aware that if you can't get to the decisionmaker, you will most assuredly get a maybe or a stall. A decisionmaker can say either yes or no. Someone who is not a decision maker can only say no. As you move up the management hierarchy, recognize that top management generally buys concepts and ideas, not nuts and bolts.

Middle or lower management usually buys what the product is or how it works. It usually does not know the big picture so it is not interested in concepts or ideas. You must sell differently at different levels.

When a middle person says, "You can give me the information, I'll pass it along." I have one approach that has worked for me: "Mr. Prospect, I have an idea that can help your firm (improve sales, save time, etc.) Do you believe that (saving time, money, etc.) is important to your management? Would you agree that the best person to give it the information would be me? Fine, let's set up an appointment."

Competition

Without competition you would eventually become complacent and ineffective. Competition is necessary for growth. Look around you. (When you must compete for a sale or position, you work harder, become smarter, and if you persist, you usually win.) I've heard many salespeople say, "I wish I had an exclusive product or service with exclusive features." If you did, I guarantee you wouldn't sell any more than you do now. You're only looking for an outside crutch when you blame your competition for your own lack of ability or creativity.

Don't run from competition. Hit it head-on. Find out where it is weak. Concentrate on your strengths and attack your competitor's weaknesses.

To hit your competition where it is vulnerable you should stress the positive features of your product that are obvious weaknesses of your competition's product. But don't hide and don't give up. That one weakness could get you the sale. If you have any weaknesses, either do something positive about them, or create a presentation that builds so well on your assets that your weaknesses won't matter.

Chapter Summary

The worst emotion in the selling profession is false hope. More people fail in sales because they don't have enough qualified prospects to talk to than for any other reason. Therefore, the tendency is to accept a "maybe" for two reasons. First, if you eliminate all your "maybes," who will you see? So, you hang on. Second, a "yes" or "no" is final. We want to hope this "maybe" will be the exception.

Selling is not a numbers game, but a quality numbers game. Just seeing enough people is no longer enough in a competitive economy.

Control is another serious problem. The prospect wants it, but to sell, you must control with tact and skill.

Learn to talk less—ask more and believe for every poor suspect you now have there are dozens of good-quality prospects waiting to hear your story and have you help them with their problems.

Chapter Problem

Your prospect is a middle manager. You know the company can use your product or service. The prospect says the company is not interested. You have a referral to his boss. How would you approach this situation?

_____
_____
_____
_____
_____
_____
_____
_____
_____
_____

Common Mistakes to Avoid

1. Accepting a "maybe" instead of a "yes" or "no." "Maybe" is a postponed "no."
2. Only playing the numbers game—seeing enough people—makes sales! How about seeing fewer but better people?
3. Letting the prospect have control.

Prospecting questions

1. What is prospecting?
2. Can you name several methods of prospecting?
3. What is the purpose of prospecting?

4. Can you name several methods of qualifying prospects?
5. What is your time worth?
6. Do you keep prospecting records?
7. Who are your best prospects?
8. What is radiation prospecting?
9. What is your best source for new prospects?
10. Why is prospecting the most important phase of selling?

There are 199 ways to beat, but only one way to win—get there first.
—Willie Shoemaker

Exercises

1. Get five referrals every day for 4 weeks.
2. Select one center and begin to develop him or her.
3. Design an opening question sequence.

Visualization Exercises

1. Actually see your prospect file full of top-caliber, qualified prospects.
2. See your next customer giving you several referrals and qualifying them for you.
3. See your center of influence calling you regularly and giving you several qualified leads.

Chapter Affirmations

I have a referral awareness. Today I will generate five referrals. My centers of influence send me several qualified prospects every month. I ask good qualifying questions and my prospects are happy to cooperate. I am a good sales prospector. I am continuously improving my prospecting ability.

Watch my dust.
—Babe Ruth

THE SALES INTERVIEW

Chapter Objectives

1. Each interview should be customized to each prospect's wants and desires.

2. Sell the prospect and educate the customer.

3. Learn how to get the prospect to sell himself.

4. Get advance commitment.

He that speaks much, is much mistaken.

—Ben Franklin

Half-wits talk much but say little.

—Ben Franklin

Introduction

You have something important to say and you are eager to get to the next prospect, so the sooner you finish your presentation, the sooner you can give another presentation. You spend your day logging presentations, playing the proverbial numbers game, OR you don't have enough prospects so you spend too much time with poorly qualified suspects until one of you runs out of time or patience.

You want to talk; you have the need to talk. You want to educate, you want to spend a lot of time with your prospects because it makes you feel comfortable or you think it makes them feel comfortable; you like to visit.

People are persuaded more by your own confidence, belief, and enthusiasm than by your logic or knowledge.

The sales presentation or interview is your vehicle to tell your story, persuade, and motivate. It is an important step and it needs the right blend of emotion, enthusiasm, logic, and knowledge.

Different people buy for different reasons. In this chapter, we'll discuss how to design a custom presentation for each of your prospects— not a canned sales talk, but a customized, flexible persuasive sales message; one that works.

Are You Guilty?

While in Mexico, Carleton Beals fell into the habit of buying two oranges from an orange woman near his house. One day, when he was planning to give a party, he undertook to buy her entire stock of four dozen oranges.

Severely, she said, "Here are your two," and handed him his usual purchase.

"But this time I want to buy all the rest of them."

"Why," she said, outraged, "you can't. What do you think I would do all the rest of the day with no oranges to sell?"

The Sales Interview

The approach: What is an interview? "A meeting at which information is obtained from a person." I would like to alter Mr. Webster's definition slightly: "A meeting at which information is exchanged between two parties." The key to a good sales presentation is a two-way exchange of information that builds interest and desire in the mind of the prospect. But a good sales presentation or interview must be based on a sound foundation.

The most important element in the entire sales process is the discovery of the dominant emotional buying motive. When you know it, the interview can be shorter, easier, more powerful, and will conclude more successfully than if you work essentially "in the dark."

The manner in which you structure the interview and the vocabulary you use, can be completely different depending on what the dominant emotional need or want is at the time.

The first step in designing our custom approach is to take a look at why people buy and why they do not buy.

People buy to satisfy wants, not needs. Needs are logical and wants are emotional. A need can become a want but a want doesn't necessarily have to be a need.

Satisfying wants will increase your sales and income. (Clerks attempt to satisfy needs.) You may have read that professional sales people are problem solvers. I think the professional salesperson is a problem creator. If people buy wants, then wants can be created by creating problems. The need may always have been there, but no action will be taken until an emotional want situation is created either by the prospect or the salesperson.

Let's analyze the emotional reasons why people do not buy: no hurry, no interest, no trust, no money, no desire, no need.

No hurry—"Why rush? Maybe I can save money, time, trouble, etc., if I wait. This is not a priority at this time." A professional salesperson makes it a top priority now. She creates a sense of urgency.

No interest—If you can't create interest you will never create desire. If you have a qualified prospect you create interest by solving a problem she did not know she had.

No trust—Before a prospect buys your product or service, she must first buy you. She must believe you, and I believe she must respect you. You must have credibility. All of these come from confidence, belief in yourself and your product, enthusiasm, and knowledge. One of the best ways to build trust is to be sincerely interested in your prospect, and her needs, wants and problems, and listen to what she has to say.

No money—Either it is an excuse, a stall, or a legitimate reason. You must know the truth before you can continue. A stall and an excuse you can handle (see Chapter Five). If it is a legitimate reason, terminate the interview.

No desire—You cannot cause desire if you don't get interest. But once you have interest, desire is easy. No desire comes from a lack of understanding how the product or service will actually satisfy the prospect's dominant emotional buying motive. If you know the motive, you can create desire.

No need—If there is no need, create a want and make the prospect feel the need emotionally. If you are going to persuade a prospect to buy your product or service for the first time or use your product to replace an existing supplier, home, auto, etc., you have to make him a little uncomfortable with his present situation. How you accomplish this is one of the subjects of this chapter.

The opening questions: Now that we have addressed why people do not buy, why do they buy? Please write the answers to the following three questions: First, why do people or companies buy from you? Second, why should they buy from you? Third, why don't they buy from you? The answers to these questions will provide you with some interesting insight into your selling behavior and clues as to areas where you need to improve.

Prospect Wants

Here is a list of twenty-five reasons why people buy. See if you can add any to the list.

1. To make money.
2. To save money.
3. To save time.
4. To avoid effort.
5. To gain comfort.
6. To achieve cleanliness.
7. To improve health.
8. To escape pain.
9. To be popular.
10. To attract the opposite sex.
11. To gain praise.
12. To conserve possessions.
13. To increase enjoyment.
14. To gratify curiosity.
15. To protect family.
16. To be in style.
17. To satisfy appetite.
18. To emulate others.
19. To have beautiful things.
20. To avoid criticism.
21. To take advantage of opportunities.
22. To be individual.
23. To avoid trouble.
24. To protect reputation.
25. To have safety.

Now let's break this list down to the eight major emotional reasons why people buy.

Prestige—I want you to think I'm important and successful, so I buy products and services that say, "Look at me." We buy homes, automobiles, club memberships, vacations, designer clothes, and so on. What products can you think of that appeal to prestige?

Love—We buy because we care. We buy security and safety fencing, smoke alarms, insurance, greeting cards, flowers, cemetery plots, candy. See how many products you can add that we buy because of love or caring.

Curiosity—People are basically curious by nature—some are more curious than others. The movie industry uses curiosity with its previews. The publishing industry with its pictures on the cover of magazines and books. What other industries can you add? How does the automobile industry use curiosity?

Imitation—We buy to copy other successful or well-known people. We want others to think we are as smart, clever, good-looking, etc. The clothing industry uses imitation. How does the jewelry industry use imitation? Can you add any to this list?

Fear—We buy many products because we fear what life would be like without them. We fear losing what we have. We fear for our future and loved ones. Here are some of the fears that cause people to buy: Fear of poverty, fear of criticism, fear of ill health, fear of loss of love, fear of loss of liberty, fear of old age, fear of death, fear of being made a fool of in front of others you know. What products do we buy because of fear?

Rivalry—Rivalry is the opposite of imitation. In imitation, we buy because someone or the group did. In rivalry, we buy because someone else or the group did not. This can be seen where companies or individuals compete.

Self Preservation—People really want to live a long time. When someone says he doesn't really want to live past age seventy, wait until he's sixty-nine, then ask him again. We buy many things because they will help us live longer or healthier; e.g., vitamins, health foods, exercise equipment, diets.

Variety—People want something new. They easily tire of the same old car, clothes, vacations. They want a little spice now and then. Why do you think the fashion industry prospers year in and year out? How about the success of fads through the years?

Complete the matching exercise (Figure 4-A) Match the product or services with two of the best emotional buying motives. Some products or services may appeal to several. But there are only one or two right answers. (See Figures 4-A & 4-B)

Great talkers should be cropped for they have no need of ears.
—Ben Franklin

Figure 4-A

Buying motives	**Answer**
Variety	_____Auto insurance
Fear	_____Self-help books
Imitation	_____Stereos
Prestige	_____Vacations
Love	_____Health insurance
Self-preservation	_____Country club membership
Curiosity	_____Lawn mower
Rivalry	_____Home
	_____Automobile
	_____Designer jeans
	_____Cross pen
	_____Alarm clock
	_____Plants
	_____Digital watch
	_____Carpet
	_____Vacation souvenirs
	_____Cameras

EIGHT BASIC EMOTIONAL REASONS WHY PEOPLE BUY

How can you sell your product or service using each one of the eight basic reasons? Initially, only a few reasons come easily to mind and then you may come to a halt. Force yourself to concentrate and get over this hump. By staying with it, ideas will begin to flow.

Of these eight reasons, there may be one major emotional reason why a prospect will buy now. It is up to you to uncover it in your initial prospecting investigation or when you go through the features and benefits of your product/service.

Not everyone is going to have the same reason to purchase. Commit these to memory so they are readily available when needed.

Figure 4-B
HOW CAN I SELL MY PRODUCT/SERVICE BY USING:

1. Prestige:
2. Imitation:
3. Curiosity:
4. Love:
5. Fear:
6. Rivalry:
7. Self-Preservation:
8. Variety:

We could also condense the list of eight reasons why people buy down into two simple emotional reasons. People buy to either gain benefits or avoid losses. Which do you think would be the stronger emotion? If you guessed to gain something you did not have, you are wrong. People are more interested in keeping what they already have than in getting something new. If they had one choice it would be to avoid losses. How can you use these emotional buying motives in designing your presentation? If you select the wrong reason to appeal to, it is almost impossible to get attention, interest, desire, and action.

Here is a step-by-step method to design a powerful, persuasive, flexible presentation. Follow each step and you will have a sales presentation that will work for you for many years.

Step one: Define product features. Features are what the product is or what the product does. It is what makes your product or service a product or service. Features are not necessarily all positive. You can have negative features. Define benefits. Benefits are what each feature does for the user of the product or services.

Make a list of all your product's features, every one—minor and major, positive and negative. (See Figure 4-C)

After you have completed this exercise, the next step is to arrange this list in two ways. First, group the features according to which of the eight emotional buying motives to which they appeal. (See Figure 4-D)

The second way to arrange the list is according to the popularity of the features (list from most to least popular).

Step two: After you have completed these exercises, write a sentence describing each feature from the customer's point of view. These should be benefit statements.

Examples:

Feature: Tilt steering wheel.

Benefit: You can move the steering wheel out of your way upon entering and leaving your automobile to make entering and departing easier.

Feature: Monthly payment plan.

Benefit: It is not necessary to have all the needed investment before purchasing.

Feature: Two bathrooms in the home.

Benefit: (You think of one!)

Feature: Service contract.

Benefit: (You think of one!)

Before we go on, you must firmly implant the following idea in your mind: People do not buy features, they buy benefits. This statement bears repeating. People do not buy features, they buy benefits. They care about what the product is, how it works, what it looks like, etc., only to the extent that they perceive those features as answering the question, "How is this going to help me solve my problems?" (See Figure 4-E)

Step three: How would you decide which feature to discuss with each prospect, or would you give each prospect all the features? Do you always know why each of your prospects is going to buy? For example, can you recall a recent sale you made because the prospect was concerned about what other people thought (prestige)? Did he buy because he needed something new? Or needed a change (variety)? See what I'm getting at?

Most salespeople literally deluge their prospects with information or features. "Our product does this and that, has this and that, our company will do this and that."

Figure 4-C

PRODUCT FEATURES

Product Name	Features

Figure 4-D

CUSTOMER BENEFITS

Feature	Benefit

Figure 4-E

Features: These are the nuts and bolts of your product or service: what it is or what it does. People don't buy features.

Benefits: End results of the features—what's in it for me. People buy what a product/service will do for them.

List of your features: From the smallest to the largest, then number them in order of their customer appeal.

Use different pivot statements: What this means to you, what you are really concerned about, what you want, etc.

Put the benefits in sentence form for each feature.

Commit this list to memory: Implant it in your subconscious, it is an important part of your presentation.

Feature	Pivot	Benefit

You don't know the prospect's emotional reason for buying, so you cover all the features hoping one will hit the "hot button." You are attempting to educate your prospect into buying. But remember, people do not buy logically, they buy emotionally, then justify the purchase logically. Your role is to sell the prospect and then, if necessary, educate him or her. Most salespeople talk too much! Are you guilty? If so, begin today to understand—talking doesn't make sales, listening does.

Giving all the features takes too much of both your time and your prospect's time. And usually when people have a lot of information on something, they tend to get confused. When they are confused, they have trouble deciding—they have to "think it over."

Only give your prospect enough information to make the sale. How do you select which information? Let's say you sell a club membership. Your prospect's dominant buying motive is love. Which features of your product would you discuss? That's right, all those features of your product that appeal to love. Let's say you sell computers and your prospect's dominant buying motive is fear. Which feature would you discuss? Yes, all those features of your product that help him solve the fear he has that originates from his problem.

Find the dominant buying motive. Then stress all the aspects of your product that appeal to that motive. How do you find the dominant buying motive? In Chapter 3 we discussed asking a number of questions before giving the presentation. Many of the answers to these questions will give you clues to the dominant buying motive. Learn to listen between the lines. You will be astonished at what you will hear and learn.

Step four: Now that we have developed a list of features and benefits, and know the dominant buying motive, let's give the presentation in such a way that we can: (1) create two-way communication, (2) get the prospect involved, (3) use as little time as possible, (4) close as early at possible, and (5) keep the prospect's attention.

The Presentation

The Opening: I suggest the following opening. It can be used with most products and services and it helps you set the proper tone for the interview:

Good morning, Ms. Prospect. Thank you for taking time today with me to share some ideas on how we can help you (insert one of the major benefits of your product, e.g., save time, improve productivity, increase sales). I don't know how my company can best be of service to you. The best way for me to determine that is for me to ask you a few questions. Is that OK? Do you mind if I take notes? According to your schedule, how much time do we have today? (See Figure 4-F)

With this approach your first remark is a question that asks permission to ask more questions.

Which questions should you ask first? There are two categories of questions; general information and then the specific information you need in order to know if you have a prospect.

First, the general questions;
1. Do they have the money?
2. Are they decision makers?
3. Will they make a decision?
4. What will their general area of interest be?
5. What will their general area of desire be?
6. Do you have favorable selling conditions?

Then the specific questions. (This list should come from your exercise in Figure 3-A, pg. 96)

The next step is to just start asking questions until you believe you have identified the real emotional buying motive. It can happen after two questions or it could take seventy-five. Each situation is different. Here is where some general common sense, horse sense and street sense will come in handy—all of these come from experience.

The Body: You are now finished with the opening of your presentation. The second part is the body. Here is where you select, based on what you learned in the opening, which features to cover.

You need to cover them in a systematic fashion. I suggest the following formula: Feature, Pivot, Product Benefit, Customer Benefit, Qualify, and Qualify.

First, you mention the feature: "One of the features of our service is a monthly payment plan..."

The Pivot: What you want, what you're interested in, what concerns you, (you don't use them all). The pivot is a bridge of words that enables you to smoothly move from a discussion of the feature to a discussion of the benefit.

Product Benefit: The product benefit is what the feature does for the product. For example, slots in an ashtray is the feature, the product benefit is it keeps the cigarettes in the ashtray.

The Customer Benefit is that you don't get burn holes on your tables or rugs (safety, cleanliness.) The customer benefit is how the product benefit benefits the customer.

Notice how the product benefit is a midway step in the understanding of the feature itself. Most people will not have the same level of understanding of your product that you do. So don't assume they do. Take them step-by-step through this discussion and you can be sure they will both hear and understand you.

The optimist proclaims that we live in the best of all possible worlds, and the pessimist fears this is true.
—James Branch Cabell

Next, the **first qualify**. At this point you should want to know both if the prospect has heard you and understands what this particular feature means to her. "Ms. Prospect, how would monthly payments help you?"; "Why would this feature be important to you?" To explain it, she has to have heard you and understood you. You are also creating a two-way communication; therefore, your presentation is not a lecture.

The **second qualify**. Let's say she doesn't really care about that feature and its subsequent benefit. You then go on to the next feature and repeat the process. On the other hand, let's say in her feedback on her understanding of the benefit, she indicates special interest in this particular feature. The second qualify then becomes a trial close. What is a trial close? It is an attempt to close the sale before you are ready for the final close.

Figure 4-F
CLIENT INTERVIEW

Person(s) interviewed	Date Interviewed	Date to follow up
_____	_____	_____
_____	_____	_____
_____	_____	_____

Company Name   Date Business Started

Address   City   State   Zip

Telephone   Ext.   Secretary/Assistant

Number of Employees   Divisions/Departments

Product or Service:

_____
_____
_____

Problems:

_____
_____
_____

Opportunities:

_____
_____
_____

Business Interests:

_____
_____
_____

Business Involvements:

_____
_____
_____

Personal Interests:

_____

_____

_____

Miscellaneous:

_____

_____

_____

Disposition:

_____

_____

_____

Figure 4-G

CLIENT HISTORY

Name:_____Company:_____
Address:_____
Telephone Number (business)_____(home)_____

Date	Action	Follow-up required

In a presentation, you should trial close early and often. For example, "Ms. Prospect, have you got yourself convinced yet that this is a solution to your problem, what you want, etc., or should I tell you more?"

One purpose of trial closes is that you get the prospect used to your asking closing type questions. By the time the final close comes, it doesn't have the same intensity that it would if you only asked one closing question. (We'll have more on this in Chapter 6.)

The second qualify, then, would go like this. "Is the monthly payment program important enough for you to go ahead today?" If the answer is "no," continue to the next feature. If "yes," close.

There you have it—a sales presentation with structure, but also sensitive to each prospect's style, problems and wants. If you will follow this format, your presentations can be shorter, more interesting and more profitable.

To summarize this section, I believe a good sales presentation has four ingredients:
1. It is brief and to the point.
2. You always speak from the prospect's point of view. Keep yourself emotionally out of the interview. Don't talk about yourself unless it contributes to the presentation. Resist the temptation to talk about your tennis game, hobbies, or personal interests.
3. The ability to listen. Most people don't listen. Remember, most of your prospects will tell you what you need to tell them to sell them, but you have to listen.
4. Get the customer involved. If anything needs to be opened, turned on, started, flipped, closed, etc., get the prospect to do it. The more you get prospects involved, the more the product or service becomes theirs in their mind.

Physical Control

Have you ever been getting ready to make an important selling point and the prospect's telephone rings? Have you ever just asked a closing question and a visitor comes in? These and many other similar circumstances can, in an instant, destroy a good sales presentation, and there is nothing you can do about it. Or is there?

First of all, you must decide what you will tolerate in an interview and what you won't. Establish your environmental rules and follow them. I ask for the prospect to ask his secretary to hold his calls. "Do you mind if I shut the door?" "May I move my chair here?" You need to set the stage the way you want it. If your prospect fights you and is not willing to cooperate, maybe this should give you a clue how the rest of the interview will go. If he or she keeps you waiting, tells you how much time you have, or wants to take control by asking you questions, you've lost control. It takes guts sometimes to stand your ground, but it's a necessary requirement if you wish to succeed. You must establish physical control. It is up to you.

Emotional Control

Do you have the will to win, a deep burning desire to succeed, to sell? You must if you ever hope to control your prospect emotionally. Be willing to change yourself and influence the situation so that the outcome is favorable.

An effective sale is a win-win situation. If anyone loses when you sell, eventually you will be the big loser. You must develop a closing attitude. You begin to close the minute you introduce yourself to your prospect, and you keep closing until you've finished.

Advice Commitment

Another important aspect of emotional control is your prospect must know from the beginning you are there to sell, not just visit. One method I use is called closing on advance commitment. The concept is, "If I can, will you? If we can, will you?" The burden of how you can or if you can is still on you, but why convince the prospect only to get to the end of the presentation and have him tell you he has to think it over, shop around, or simply can't afford it now. If you had tried, you probably could have moved these excuses to the beginning. It is just as easy to solve them at the beginning as it is at the end. The difference is, if you can't solve them at the beginning, why bother to even give your presentation? On the other hand, if you can successfully solve them in the beginning, imagine how easy the actual close will be. You don't have to solve them later.

How do you close on advance commitment? You have just completed your opening questions and have determined that you have a prospect worthy of your time. Proceed as follows:

"Mr. Prospect, I appreciate your cooperation and honest answers to my questions. I have only three more. Is that OK?"

First Question

"Let's pretend for a minute that you have seen the idea I have to help you (increase sales, save time, etc.). I've completed my presentation. You like the program and believe it will solve your problem. Would anyone else need to be consulted in the decision process or can you make the decision yourself?" If he says, "No," he has to consult someone—wife, partner, whoever—then ask: "Is there any reason why they can't join us now?" If the other person is not available, say, "When would he be available? Fine, let's reschedule our meeting for next week." (Whatever the situation requires.) The prospect will agree, the suspect will try to convince you to give your presentation anyway.

If he says, "He can join us," say, "Fine, let's do it." If he says, "I can make the decision myself," then proceed.

Second Question

"Mr. Prospect, let's assume for a minute that you believe I have a solution to your problem and you are convinced that it will work and that the investment is fair. Would there be any reason why you couldn't make a decision today?" If he says he can't make the decision today, find out why and solve the problem before you go on. Resist the tendency to give your presentation unless you are completely satisfied you will get some action today, either a "yes" or a "no."

Third Question

"Mr. Prospect, if you are convinced beyond any shadow of a doubt that we have an effective, reasonably-priced solution to your need, can you invest $_____?" Pick a number that fairly represents what you have determined will do the job for him. I even pad this amount in the beginning a little. He is, if he goes along, prepared for this level of investment. When you get to the close and tell him you can solve his problem for less, he'll feel as though he is getting a bargain.

Using this method, you can smoke out your suspects early. Keep in mind that there are exceptions to every rule—the method we've been discussing doesn't always work. However, don't let exceptions rule your selling style.

The pursuit of truth shall set you free—even if you never catch up with it.
—Clarence Darrow

Negative Words to Avoid

1. Deal—use opportunity.
2. Sell, sold—use involve.
3. Buy—use own.
4. Pitch—use presentation, demonstration.
5. Cost—price use total investment.
6. Down payment—use initial or first investment.
7. Monthly payment—use monthly investment.
8. Contract—use agreement, paperwork, forms.
9. Sign—use authorize, OK, witness my signature, approve, endorse.

Some Irritating Habits to Avoid

1. Talking too much.
2. Interrupting.
3. Not looking at the person.
4. Never smiling.
5. Fidgeting.
6. Tapping fingers, pen or pencil.
7. Asking a question about what was just said.
8. Putting words in the other person's mouth.
9. Arguing with everything.
10. Constantly looking at the time.
11. Smoking.
12. Saying, "Do you know what I mean?" "Do you understand?"
13. Always being dogmatic.
14. Anticipating what the other person is going to say.

15. Always overstating the facts or stretching the truth.
16. Not remembering names and faces.
17. Knocking your competitor.
18. Not using showmanship, conducting a boring presentation. Make it an event, be remembered, do something startling.
19. Having poor personal hygiene—Body odor, bad breath, sloppy shoes or clothes, poorly groomed hair, dirty hands or fingernails. If you've got problems here, straighten them out today.
20. Not believing in what you are selling or doing.

The First Fifteen Minutes

Was it a comedy? A tragedy? A monologue or a documentary? A hit? Or was the show canceled? We are not talking about the latest effort from Hollywood or New York but your last sales presentation.

There are three ways to evaluate the success of any sales presentation. Let's continue for a moment with our movie example. Before the script finds its way to your local movie theater, there have been hours of planning and organization, preparation, and execution—the actual filming.

In every profession, there are these same three steps, whether it is a doctor preparing for surgery, a builder building a house, or a parent planning the next meal. There is always some degree of planning, preparation, and then execution. The success of the outcome or finished product depends on the effectiveness of all three. The sales process is no exception.

The planning or organizing is the pre-call research, investigation, and general information gathering. The organization is deciding the strategy for the call, not planning the information that will be delivered but the sequence of events. The execution is what you say and do once in the prospect's domain. The focus of this section is on the execution; however, it is necessary to cover some of the key points that should have been addressed in the first two steps if the actual presentation strategy, dynamics, and outcome are to be understood and successful.

The sales process is a series of relationships—not just personal relationships but the relationship between the elements of the process. The first element is your attitudes about, perceptions of, and beliefs on values and judgments, and their impact on every aspect of the process itself.

This element, more than any other, will determine your success and/or failure in selling. The next element is prospecting. That's where you get information. Next is the sales presentation, where you give information and answer sales resistance. Then comes the close. Last is servicing the client for repeat and/or referral business. The success of the sales presentation is a function of your effectiveness of managing your attitudes and the timeliness and accuracy of the information you receive.

Have you ever had a prospect say to you, "You have fifteen minutes to convince me that I should give you anymore of my valuable time." Well, if they don't say it, you can bet they are thinking it.

We are going to assume that you have what you believe is a good prospect, and you are now in the prospect's office ready to begin. It's show time.

The goals or objectives of the first fifteen minutes follow:

—Build a positive rapport.

—Establish an atmosphere of trust and respect.

—Gain control of the sales process.

—Fill in the gaps of specific prospect information that you have not learned to this point.

—Confirm the accuracy of previous information gained.

—Uncover prospect prejudices, needs, desires, attitudes, opinions, problems, and potential resistance.

—Discover the dominant emotional buying motive.

—Determine the urgency and their willingness to proceed now.

—Determine whether you are in the presence of the decision maker, or discover who the additional people are who should be involved.

—Sell them on the need for additional time to deliver the balance of your presentation.

That's a lot to do in just fifteen minutes, but there is one selling skill that can accomplish all of these in the time allotted—the ability to ask the right questions in the right way at the right time.

There are two basic types of questions you want to use in the early stages of the sales process. They are open- and closed-ended questions. Closed-ended questions are used to verify specific attitudes and get answers to specific information requests. For example, "What equipment are you currently using? Who is your present supplier?" Open-ended questions are used to query the prospects feelings, attitudes, opinions, prejudices, and judgments. For example, "How do you feel about the service you are getting from your current supplier? What has been your experience with our type of product or service?" Remember, closed-ended questions cut off dialogue, and open-ended questions encourage dialogue. Information is power. Questions help you prevent lost sales by getting you important information about your prospect before you "deliver" your sales message. They will help you to focus on only those features that are of interest or concern to the buyer.

Generally speaking, you want to use more open-ended questions in the early portion of the sales process. If you use a closed-ended question early, follow it immediately with an open-ended question. You want to get the prospect talking, and you want to keep them talking.

An opening I have used for over twenty years is, "I don't know how I can best be of service to you or your organization, the best way for me to determine that is if I can ask you a few questions. Is that OK?"

This strategy accomplishes two critical things in the early part of the presentation. First, it gets you control of the sales process, and second, it gives you permission to get as much information as you can and need early. Keep in mind, the person who asks the questions controls the conversation, and the person who talks the most dominates it. In a sales presentation, which do you think would be the most effective strategy?

Remember, your prospects are constantly asking themselves "Why should I give you more time?" Questions keep their focus on their needs, problems, concerns, and off of your products, features, and selling style. It also shows the prospect you are more interested in them than you are in just selling something—anything—to them. One of the best ways to build trust and rapport in any relationship is by being more interested in the other person than in yourself.

This particular opening also helps to get and maintain the prospect's attention by breaking through their preoccupation with the many other issues they have on their plate.

There are a few concepts you should consider, however, before you continue with your presentation.

One. Never cover price until you have had an opportunity to build value. Price will always seem high if value is perceived as low. The way you build value is to relate the features and benefits of your product and/or service to the specific needs, desires, or problems of the prospect. The time for building value is after you know what these are. If you introduce price too soon, you will end up in a price-alone battle. An early request for a price is a signal that you have a poor prospect or one that will buy on price alone. The way to disarm a price request too early is to say something like, "I am sure price is a concern to you. Are you only interested in price, or is service, quality, reputation, etc., also important to you?"

Two. I would rather leave early in the process with a "no," than go through the entire process and get a "maybe." With a no, I know where I stand. With a maybe, I have only false hope. And after more than thirty years in selling, my experience is that most "maybes" end up "nos." If you terminate an interview, be sure to leave a prospect and not an enemy behind. One way to accomplish this is to say, "Mr. Prospect, your answers to my questions have indicated that this is not a good time to be discussing our product or service. Allow me to get back to you in six months to see how your circumstances have changed."

Three. Timing is everything in selling. Remember, people buy when they are ready to buy, not when you need to sell. Attempting to force a prospect to buy when you need to sell is what we commonly call the hard sell.

Back to the Presentation

Your opening question and your follow-up questions will determine how much more time your prospect will allow you. Poor questions, and you'll be out of there. Good questions, and you can stay as long as you need to determine whether you have a prospect that is worth more of your time. The critical thing to remember is that you are not selling your product or service in this early stage. You are earning the right to take more of their time later.

Let's relate this entire scenario to that of visiting your doctor for stomach problems. If doctors prescribed a prescription right after your informing them of your symptoms, I doubt if you would take their advice. They need information, and they get it from a patient history, exam, x-rays, and so on. Once they feel confident they see the big picture, they are ready to give a diagnosis, and you will be more receptive to it. What if, after you were in their office, they said you have only fifteen minutes for us to decide on your medical fate! I would bet you would find another doctor. What if the doctors spent their entire time telling you about their education, experience, successes, personal philosophies, etc.? That is not why you are there. That is not why you are in the prospect's office. You are there to get information, not give it. There will be time for that in the second segment of the sales process.

Let's summarize with a few basic sales rules.

One. Your prospect will tell you what you need to tell them to sell them.

Two. The information you don't get soon enough will hurt you later in the process.

Three. Just because the prospect will see you doesn't mean they are a good prospect now.

Four. People buy from people they trust, not people they like.

Five. Your role is to sell the prospect, then educate your customer, not educate prospects and sell customers.

Six. You will never close a sale on a poor prospect with a good product, good sales presentation, or tricky close; however, a well-qualified prospect will help you sell them.

The first fifteen minutes are like building the foundation of a house. Get the foundation right and the rest of the construction will be successful.

Presentation Odds and Ends

The following information needs to be covered briefly, but doesn't generally fit in with the material we've covered up to this point. So, here is a list and a short explanation of each point.

1. **Never argue with your prospect.** You may win the argument, but lose the sale. However, if he is arguing about something that is detrimental to your product and his argument is based on a lie or a half-truth, it needs to be addressed. But, don't you be the one to defend his position. Let him defend his own lie. Just start

asking him a series of questions. "Where did you hear that?" "When did you hear it last?" "Do you feel that the information is compatible with the other things you now know about our service?" Sooner or later, if his information is incorrect, he will admit that it really isn't important or it's only hearsay.

2. **Work from appointments** as often as possible and schedule your appointments at least a week in advance. If you want to be thought of as a pro—sell like a pro. When you cold call, that communicates that you really don't have a busy schedule. The prospect may think, "Maybe you're not good enough, knowledgeable enough, to help me."

3. **Develop a strong "as if" assumptive attitude** during the presentation. Use words like when (When we deliver your program. When your ad appears. When your membership card arrives) where (Where would we deliver your samples? Where would we ship your merchandise?); who (Who would be responsible for implementation? Whom would we contact for service? Who will be responsible for the payments?); how (How will you use this model? How will you decorate this room?); your (We've used "your" in almost every example); what (What would you do with the excess copies? What would you do with an increase in income?). If you are giving a presentation to a suspect, he will object to your assumptive words and attitudes, and resist you each time. This is an excellent tool to determine if the prospect is buying and going along with you. A prospect will cooperate and not mind your assumptions because it is his intent to do business. This can help you weed out your suspects early.

4. **Plan each call.** Each prospect is different, each situation or problem is unique. Planning can pay huge dividends. Just take a few minutes and think through the sales presentation before you actually give it—what you'll say, what you would like the prospect to say, how you will act and how he or she will react.

5. **The Hidden vs. the Real Person.** Most people have two reasons for their actions and words. There is the real reason and

then the reason they give. You cannot effectively sell to the given reasons. You must get beneath the surface to the real reasons. For example, "The price is too high" (given); "My credit isn't good enough to qualify" (real); "I have to think it over" (given); "You haven't convinced me that I should take action now" (real).

6. **What do you think or feel?** Never ask prospects what they think about something. Thinking is logical. Ask how they feel about something.

7. **Know your business.** How knowledgeable are you about your company's products, policies, history, goals and purpose? In fifty words or less, try writing a description of each of these areas.

8. **Know your competition.** Have you ever lost a sale to a competitor? Did you really know why? I believe you should know as much about your competition as you do about your own company. Not only the company, but its salespeople as well as its practices. This can help you stress your strengths in comparison to their weaknesses.

9. **How to terminate.** During the presentation, once you discover, for whatever reason, that you no longer have a prospect, you should terminate the interview and go on to your next prospect. Terminate professionally. Leave a suspect behind, not an enemy. "Ms. Prospect, because of this information you have given me, your current circumstances, lack of interest (use whatever you feel comfortable with), I don't believe that I can be of service to you at this time. Permit me to get back to you at some point in the future to see if your situation has changed. Thank you for your time, honesty and courtesy. Goodbye."

10. **Practice.** How good do you think the Dallas Cowboys would be if they just showed up for games? How about the Boston Celtics? How well would Bruce Jenner or Mark Spitz have done if they only showed up for meets—how about Jimmy Connors or Jack Nicklaus? The pros practice.

Most salespeople practice on their best prospects, if at all. Are you just showing up for the games and expecting to win? How do you practice in sales? It's easy. You practice a new technique, idea or method on a spouse, associate, friend, or supervisor.

If you want to be a pro—practice, practice, practice.

Lord, deliver me from the man who never makes a mistake, and also from the man who makes the same mistake twice.

—William J. Mayo

Chapter Summary

A good sales presentation gets the prospect involved as often and as much as possible, is brief and to the point, and focuses on the prospect's point of view.

Keeping yourself out of the presentation emotionally is also important. If you are a sympathetic person, sympathy for your prospect will prevent a good presentation and close. If you can't afford the product, don't assume the prospect can't afford it.

Develop the habit of giving the prospect only enough information to make the sale. Remember, people buy emotionally and justify the buying decision logically.

In the sales process you must get attention, create interest, cause desire, and get action.

Chapter Problem

You are in the middle of a presentation and suddenly realize you're in over your head; however, the competition is in the waiting room and a decision must be made today. What would you do?

Common Mistakes to Avoid

1. Talking too much.
2. Not listening actively.
3. Being guilty of annoying habits.
4. Substituting product knowledge for enthusiasm.

Questions

1. What is the main objective of a good presentation?
2. How long should a good presentation take?
3. Why are questions important?
4. What are the main steps in the presentation?
5. When should you terminate a presentation?
6. Are you guilty of overtalking?
7. Are you guilty of overselling?
8. What are the qualities of a good listener?
9. What is a buying signal?
10. Do you always stick to the truth no matter how hard it hurts?

Write injuries in dust—benefits in marble.

—Ben Franklin

Exercises

1. Practice listening every day for 30 minutes.
2. Get every prospect involved.
3. Tailor your presentation to each prospect's dominant buying motive.

Visualization Exercises

Practice an effective sales presentation in your mind three times a day: One in which you say and do everything just right and your prospect also says and does everything just as you would like.

Chapter Affirmations

I am confident and enthusiastic as I give my sales presentations. My prospects are eager to hear my sales story. My prospects are anxious to buy from me. They are enthusiastic and interested in my product or service.

Winning tastes good.

—Jean-Claude Killy

HANDLING 5 OBJECTIONS

Chapter Objectives

1. How to use sales objections as sales tools.

2. How to disarm sales objections.

3. How to solve price and "think it over."

4. How to eliminate sales objections.

5

He that won't be counselled, can't be helped.

—Ben Franklin

The things which hurt, instruct.

—Ben Franklin

Introduction

Can you really sell without sales objections? The sales objection gives you the ability to know how you are doing and where you are going, right or wrong. Sales objections are necessary selling tools.

The sales pros encourage rather than run from sales objections. Losers have been hearing the same objections for years and have never done anything about them.

What is your attitude toward sales objections? When someone says, "Your price is too high," or "I want to think it over," do you give up? In this chapter we will guide you through an understanding of sales objections so you will never fear them again.

The Truth Behind Sales Objections

What are sales objections? Are they really objections? What do people have to really object about? Do most prospects expect 100 percent satisfaction in what they buy, or are they willing to sacrifice some items?

I do not believe the perfect product or service has ever been designed or developed. Terms are not right, colors are not right, sizes are too big or too small, products are too advanced or not advanced enough, they become outdated too soon or last too long. The potential list of small or large dissatisfactions is endless.

I do not believe you can fully solve all of these to the prospect's complete satisfaction. There are product imperfections, people imperfections, breakdowns in communications, rumors and more.

The key in my mind is not to create the perfect product in the prospect's mind, but rather to satisfy his obvious concerns or questions. That's the key to understanding objections. They are not really customer objections but customer questions.

For example:

Objection: I want to think it over.

The real question: Why should I buy?

Objection: I have to shop around.

The real question: Why is your product a better value?

Objection: The price is too high.

The real question: How will I benefit if I act now?

Apply this technique to any objection you get and you soon will discover and believe objections are questions in disguise.

The prospect is not saying, "I won't buy because it's too small, too old, too fast, too slow, too short, too high," but, "Can I solve my problem, need or want with it the way it is? I want it to solve my problem. Show me how it will."

When you visit a doctor, you want him to find out what is wrong with you, don't you? Then you want him to prescribe a solution that will work for you. When you need medication or surgery, you don't say, "Well, doctor, I don't think I'll take that medicine because it's the wrong color and I don't like the taste."

There Are No Such Things as Sales Objections, There Are Only Sales Questions

The first step in effectively answering all sales objections is to eliminate the word "objection" from your selling vocabulary. The second step is to understand why objections are important. They help determine prospect interest, test prospect understanding, get prospect involvement, and secure prospect acceptance.

When a prospect objects to something and you answer his objection, you develop a combative relationship. He'll come up with a new objection and when you answer that he'll find still another objection.

You start to play psychological ping pong. Who gets tired first, you or the prospect? Or who runs out of time first, you or the prospect? Looking at sales objections as negative is a losing proposition.

What's the solution? Create a consultative relationship. The prospect is not objecting but asking. You are not answering objections but questions. You must convince yourself that objections are really questions.

In this chapter, we will refer to sales objections as sales questions.

The Role of Sales Questions

When a prospect asks a question (objects), he is looking for any number of things. Here is a partial list:

1. Will it do the job I'm paying it to do?
2. Will it last?
3. Do I deserve it?
4. Can I afford it now or in the future?
5. What will other people think of my purchase?
6. If I shop around, can I get a better price?
7. I bought something like this last year and I was sorry.
8. Is the company reputable?
9. Can I trust this salesperson?
10. Why should I change suppliers?

Before you can sell over or around a prospect's questions, you must first know what they are. You must get the prospect to communicate with you. A prospect that sits deadpan for thirty minutes is difficult to sell

because he gives you no verbal clue to test against the non-verbal messages you are receiving. You must have this feedback to sell effectively.
Without it, you are selling in the dark.

Traditionally, salespeople resist or fear sales questions. They think
they are negative and would like to try to sell without them. Think of
taking a trip around the country without a map. Sooner or later you will
have to ask questions to reach your destination. The prospect is doing
the same thing. He wants to reach a favorable destination—owning your
product, but he needs some of his basic questions answered—especially
the ones you did not anticipate.

Questions from the prospect are necessary selling tools. Rather than
fear them, let's encourage them and deal with them in a confident, professional way. Questions can come up at different times in the sales
process. The timing of the question can also give you a clue as to
whether it it a legitimate question or a buying signal. For example: The
prospects have just entered the living room of a home they are consid-
ering buying. This is their first time in the home and the first room they
have seen. The prospect asks, "Do the drapes come with the home?" An
hour later, they have seen all the rooms and like the home but ask, "Do
the drapes come with the home?" Do you think their interest or question each time meant the same thing?

How about selling an auto club membership? When you start the presentation, the prospect asks, "Does the coverage include running out of
gas?" Ten minutes later, after you have completed your presentation, he
repeats the question. Do you think his motives at each time were the same?
In the first example, the prospect was probably curious. In the second case,
this question was more likely motivated from a different perspective.

I am referring to attention, interest, desire and action. In the first
example, the questions were from a prospect in the attention stage but
the same questions later may indicate a prospect in the desire stage. Be
sensitive to the differences—the questions need a different answer or
approach. Think about it for a minute. The same question, different
times, different meaning, requiring a different answer. You need sales
questions to sell.

Types of Questions

We write our own destiny…we become what we do.
—Madame Chiang Kai-Shek

Here are some of the different kinds of questions that you are going to face:

Trivial—meaning insignificant, unimportant or meaningless. What is a trivial question? Examples would be: I don't like the shade of blue on that equipment; I don't like the layout of the dash in that car. These and other questions could be important to the prospect, or they could also be trivial things to throw you off the track, or disarm your confidence. When you believe the question is really trivial (a little experience will help here) my suggestion is to acknowledge it and then ignore it. For example, "Mr. Prospect, I'm glad you brought up the color of that equipment. I plan to go into that a little later, is that okay with you?" Acknowledge it and then do not go into it later.

What if the same trivial question comes up a second time? Maybe it is not trivial. Here is how I handle that. Acknowledge it again and then either deal with it then or postpone it until you have completed your current discussion. "Mr. Prospect, I'm glad you brought that up again. (Acknowledges it a second time in such a way that the prospect is aware that you did not forget). Obviously, the color is very important to you. Let's go into that area now." (Or next depending on your discussion.) After completely discussing it, ask, "Does that completely settle that in your mind now?"

Hopeless—is just that—hopeless. For example, the prospect just bought one yesterday, has no money or credit. Pack it up and go on to the next prospect.

Unstated—Many times, the prospect says one thing and means another, such as, "The price is too high," instead of "I do not understand a particular feature of the product." If you attempt to answer the given question, the real or hidden question remains. You must smoke out the unstated question. One way is to ask the prospect, "In addition to that, are there any other questions in the back of your mind?" Most of the time the prospect has not taken the time to think about two phony reasons (most salespeople accept the first one) so this method will uncover the real question.

Another approach would be to use a simple technique at the beginning of the sales presentation that would go something like this: "Mr. Prospect, before I get into my presentation, let's get all the possible reasons why we couldn't do business out in the open from the beginning." Then help him list the reasons (the more the better—you want them all). Usually, after this exercise you will have on the sheet of paper what you need to cover to sell to this prospect.

Hearsay—Hearsay is rumor. "That model falls apart." "You don't give good service." What the prospect is really saying is, "Is what I've heard true?" She is in essence asking you a question. Answer the question. What if the problem is a real one? Solve the problem or learn to sell around your product weakness or shortcomings. Let's say for example, you are the highest-priced product in your market among all your competitors. More often than not, the prospect brings up your high price. You must now defend your position from a position of weakness. A better method would be for you, the salesperson, to bring up the negative points before your prospect does. This exhibits confidence on your part, because of your willingness to discuss your problems, negatives, or shortcomings, in an up-front manner. This also tells him you are honest because you are willing for him to know both the good and the bad. Keep in mind I said to bring up the negative points, in this case, high price, before your prospect does. When you bring up a negative or potential problem and solve it, it cannot come up again later. You therefore control when and how the negative aspects of your product are discussed. This is the straightforward approach and in my experience will produce more trust and confidence on the part of the prospect and will result in more sales.

Genuine—A genuine question is one that is real for that particular prospect at that particular time. We will discuss four methods to deal with genuine questions later in this chapter.

Prejudice—Is a prejudicial question based on logic or emotion? Yes, it's based on emotion and must be dealt with in an emotional way. Using logic does not work because the question springs not from logical feelings, but from emotional prejudice or conditioning. For example: "I never charge anything;" "I never buy Ford;" "I never buy from women;" "I don't like ranch style." The list of emotional prejudices toward buying certain products and in certain ways goes on and on.

Why do most salespeople attempt to use logic when answering prejudice or emotional questions? Usually because they do not know any better or do not know the prospect's dominant buying motive and therefore must rely on logic. If most people bought logically, this would be an excellent approach, but most buying is done emotionally. Learn to sell emotion and answer questions using the dominant buying emotion of the prospect. The only effective way to answer an emotional question is by offering an appeal to a higher buying emotion. Let's say the prospect's dominant buying motive is prestige. He wants the product, can afford it, and would benefit from its use. But his question is, "I don't need a membership. I've never had an automobile problem in my life." (Either he's lying or he's the world's luckiest person). But his question is a prejudice type, based on previous conditioned belief, not based on current reality.

The logical way to answer this question would be to give him all the reasons why his membership would prove valuable to him. But you see, his emotional prejudice is, "I won't ever need those, I never have." The emotional way to answer this question could go like this: Let's assume his dominant buying motive is prestige, "Mr. Prospect, imagine for just a minute that you are on your way to work and you have a flat tire three blocks from your office. Picture two different scenes if you would. Scene one: There you are in your newly pressed $300 suit changing a tire, stopping now and then to say hello to fellow executives as they pass by and offer assistance. Or scene two: same situation, but this time there is an AAA truck and mechanic changing your tire as you read the morning paper." Notice how this illustration appealed to his prestige?

What if his emotional buying motive had been fear? You could use the same story but you might mention in scene one the grease on his pants, dirty shoes, or a ripped jacket. Notice how we never really answered his original question, you don't have to. If it's a question that needs a logical technical answer, give it to him, but learn to recognize the difference between prejudice questions and logical questions.

Put off, delay, or stall—Many times, a prospect wants his problem solved, his wants satisfied, or his needs met. But he just doesn't want to take action now. We are an impatient society. We want everything now. We do not want to wait. So when the prospect tells you he wants to wait, he is just not convinced as to the benefits for action now. Later in this chapter we will deal with the stall which is nothing more than a version of the "I want to think it over" question.

When answering your prospect's sales questions, also learn to phrase your answer from their behavioral style. Learn to speak their language.

You will do foolish things, but do them with enthusiasm.

—Colette

Developing Answers to Your Common Sales Questions

What is your most frequently asked sales question? "Price too high?" "Think it over?" When you get that particular question or whatever your most common question is, what do you say? What are the next words out of your mouth?

_____

_____

_____

_____

I could tell you horror stories about salespeople who have been in the business for ten and twenty years and have been hearing, "I have to think it over" and have yet to come up with an effective answer. My question is, "How much longer must you hear it before you are going to do something about it?" In this book, you will not find pat answers to all your sales questions. I will give you four systems to help you develop your own answers. Giving pat answers is one of the fallacies in sales training. What works for me may not work for you. You may put a twist on what works for me to improve it to make it work better for you. If I gave you answers, you would not use them. If you develop your own, they will work for you as mine have worked for me.

System I - Step one: Make a list of every sales question (objection) you have ever heard.

Step two: Prioritize that list. (See Figure 5-A) What is the most frequent question you have ever heard, the second most frequent, and so on.

Step three: Opposite each question, develop a response that effectively answers that question. Write out the actual words and create a sentence.

Step four: Memorize the answers.

Step five: The next time you hear that particular question, use the answer you have developed. If it works, keep using it. If it does not, go back to step three and write out a new answer. Repeat steps four and five for each question until you have an effective answer for every question you ever get. Not a cute answer that you stole from me, but one that, through trial and error and practice, you developed for yourself.

Imagine how confident you would be going into every sales presentation, confident that you had an objective and an answer to every sales question you have ever heard. Instead of saying to yourself as you begin your presentation "I hope this prospect doesn't object to my price," you say yourself, "I hope this prospect brings up price—I've got this one." The opposite is also true. How do you feel going into sales presentations unsure and lacking confidence in your ability to deal with common questions you hear everyday?

System II: Turning objections into questions in the mind of the prospect. When a prospect asks a sales question—"The price is too high," or "I want to think it over," etc.—follow with these steps:

Step one: Restate his remark in the form of a question. "I believe there is a very good question in the back of your mind. I believe the question you are asking is, "Why is the investment in this product so high and is it worth it for me to make that investment? Is that your question?" If it's yes, go on to step two. If it's no, then ask, "Exactly what is the question in the back of your mind?" You will be amazed how many times the prospect will come back with, "My question is…" The purpose of this system is to get the prospect to understand that he is asking questions, not giving objections.

Step two: "Just suppose you could convince yourself that the price (investment) was reasonable, not too high. What would it take for you to convince yourself?"

Step three: "If you could convince yourself that the price was reasonable, would there be any other reason why you couldn't make a favorable decision today?"

System III-Step one: Listen carefully to the entire question. Don't think, "I've heard this one a thousand times" and turn off the prospect. Most prospects will tell you what you need to tell them to sell them if you will listen.

Step two: Sell him his own objection. Look a little defeated. (You have to be a little bit of an actor to succeed in this business.) Say, "As I see it, you are questioning why our price is so high." (Act like you are licked and are giving up.)

Step three: Confirm that this question is the only question standing in the way to your doing business today. "In addition to the price is there any other reason why we couldn't do business together today?"

Step four: Question his question. "Mr. Prospect, why do you feel so strongly about this price issue?" (Let him answer.)

Step five: "Suppose you could convince yourself that the price was reasonable. What would you need to convince yourself?"

Step six: Give him the answer memorized from your list in Figure 5-A.

Step seven: Confirm your answer. "Does that completely settle that in your mind now?"

Step eight: Close the sale.

System IV -The reverse. Turn the prospect's question into a reason to buy now. For example: "The price is just too high." Answer with, "Are you interested in quality, Mr. Prospect?" "Why are you interested in quality?" "Do you believe in using cheap materials, labor, etc.? We could give you the quality product you deserve. How many times have you seen a cheaper substitute unable to do the job or not provide the service when necessary?"

You must learn day by day, year by year, to broaden your horizon. The more things you love, the more you are interested in, the more you enjoy, the more you are indignant about—the more you have left when anything happens.
—Ethel Barrymore

Figure 5-A

Sales Question	Answer

The Two Major Questions

Let's talk about the two most common sales questions and what you can do about them.

Price is too high. Why does the prospect object to price? For one of several reasons: pride, greed, personal justification, insecurity, getting fair price, get a better price, poor credit, actually no money, like to negotiate everything, looking for a deal, has the money but not for you or your product. At any moment of stress, anxiety, or pressure, prospects tend to move to better quality to avoid risk. The bitterness of poor quality remains long after the sweetness of low price is forgotten. When someone objects to price, follow this safe rule: People rarely refuse to buy because of price. What they are saying is, "You have not convinced me that the product is worth what you are asking me to pay for it." Don't depend on price to sell—sell more quality. Generally, people do not want the cheapest price, but rather the best value for their dollar. (See Figure 5-B)

If a prospect asks you for your price before you have a chance to build value, the price will always seem high no matter how low it is. Some prospects will attempt to convince you that they are buying on price alone but don't ever believe it. Price is hardly ever the most important factor. The prospect, however, many times convinces salespeople that it is his only concern. But, remember, when you win a sale by price, you may also lose a client by price. Win clients by quality service and a good value for their investment.

It is always easier, in my opinion, to sell high quality rather than low price. When you lower price, you lower value. When you raise price, you increase value. Price will always seem high if there is no value in the prospect's mind. The way to sell against price resistance is to increase value. When a prospect objects to price, you can do one or more of the following:

1. Get back to selling the benefits of your product.
2. Reassure the prospect he is getting a quality product at a fair price.
3. Stress how this product is a solution to his problem and that it's not the price of the product that is important, but the solution itself.

4. Stress how the product satisfies his dominant buying motive.
5. Show the prospect how the product will help him avoid a loss or gain a benefit.
6. Ask him if he's looking for the cheapest product or the best value for his investment.
7. Tell him that someone or some company somewhere will always be cheaper.
8. Tell him that he is not buying for just today but for the long term. Show him how to amortize his investment over a long period of time. "This will only cost you thirty cents a day," etc.
9. Ask, "Are you interested in good quality or just enough to last or get by for today?"
10. Ask, "If you were building our product or service would you prefer to scrimp on quality to offer a low price or build the best that you could and then offer it at a fair price?"
11. When he tells you the price is too high, repeat, "the price is too high?" right back to him in the form of a question. The purpose of this method is to put the burden of defense on him. He thinks the price is too high, you don't. Let him sell his position to you. When he questions the price, why should you suddenly get on the defensive?
12. Stress that if he pays too little and it doesn't do the job, he would have to buy it again, which, of course, ends up increasing the price significantly.
13. Ask him to consider for a minute if he were selling your product would he rather sell it at a low price, high price, or fair price? Most prospects will choose fair price!

When you answer his price question, close the sale.

In Chapter Six we will cover some additional ideas for dealing with the price problem.

It is a very funny thing about life: if you refuse to accept anything but the best you often get it

—W. Somerset Maugham

Think It Over

Do you really believe that when prospects tell you they are going to think something over that they really ever do? Actually, most people have already done a great deal of thinking before actually seeing a salesperson. That's why you're there.

My philosophy has always been: If the prospect knows what business I'm in and he'll see me, he's bought. Why would he spend his valuable time with me? In reality, he has thought it over and only wants me to help him convince himself that it's OK to buy and buy now. Unfortunately, many salespeople believe that when the prospect says he's going to think it over, he actually is.

There are always exceptions you may find here and there, a prospect who will think your proposal over and decide to buy and call you. There is only one problem. If you are relying on those sales to succeed, you certainly wouldn't want to pressure anyone. By the way, you don't pressure prospects, prospects put pressure on themselves because of their wants, needs, or problems—you're there to relieve the pressure. You probably won't be in the business by the time the prospect thinks it over.

The other problem is that your competition isn't sitting idly by as you wait for your prospect's decision.

If you must assume, assume that the prospect has no intention of thinking it over. You see, prospects don't want to say no. It's too final, so they say, "Ill think it over," just in case.

Another thing to recognize is that your prospect wants to be kind to you. When he gives a no, he is rejecting your product and you as a salesperson (in his mind). He really doesn't want to hurt your feelings or reject you. So he says, "I'll think it over," and thinks to himself, "Please, just go away quietly. Don't make me say no."

Usually, when a prospect says, "I want to think it over," he is really saying, "I'm not convinced about something," or "I have an unanswered question or problem." Rather than give you the truth (perhaps its a question he'd feel stupid asking), he says, "I want to think it over." But unless you can get at the real unanswered question, you will be unable to close the sale or keep the sale closed once it has been made.

When dealing with these unknown questions, there are a few things you should clearly understand. First, prospects don't know your presentation. They think. "Is this something I should ask or is he going to cover this later?" Then, when you don't cover it, it remains unanswered. Second, if you answer all these questions as they come up, your presentation loses its form and continuity and becomes disjointed. This jumping around can cause you to not cover aspects of your product that you should, again leaving unanswered questions in the prospect's mind.

What if the same "I want to think it over" objection comes up frequently? Why not build it into your sales presentation? Disarm your prospects before they have a chance to tell you that they want to think it over. Tell them during the presentation that many people who said they wanted to think it over for various reasons (you supply the reasons), later said that they wished they had taken immediate action.

Another problem to consider is your honesty. During your presentation you tell a prospect what your product will do for him. If he says, "I want to think it over," and you agree to let him, many times that communicates to the prospect, "He says his product will solve my problem, but he doesn't believe it enough to convince me that it will do it now. Maybe it won't do it at all."

Here are a few answers that you might want to consider when the prospect says he wants to think it over.

1. Ask the prospect, "I'm sure you don't just want to think about it haphazardly, but wisely. Is that correct? Most scientific research indicates that after seventy-two hours more than 80 percent of the facts in any situation are no longer available to us for current conscious decisions. Mr. Prospect, you want to make the best decision possible, don't you? Doesn't it make sense that now when you have all the facts clear in your mind would be the best time to make the best decision for your future?"

2. "Mr. Prospect, obviously you wouldn't take the time to think this over unless you were really interested, would you? You' re not saying that just to get rid of me, are you? Just to clarify my thinking about your question, what is it about my product that you wish to consider further? Is it the color, the size, the payment structure?" The point here is to summarize the points of your presentation in such a way that you are gradually eliminating, item by item, everything that the prospect could consider.

Remember I said earlier that when a prospect says, "I want to think it over," it was because there was some unanswered question or problem? This method is designed to get at the real question or problem—to isolate it so you can then answer it.

How about the straightforward approach? "Mr. Prospect, I'm sure you have a very good reason for wanting to think more about this. Would you mind sharing it with me?" You can always use the old standby, "Many people feel as you do—that thinking things over is a good method. In fact, I felt that way at one time, but most successful people I know found that it is better to make a decision when all the facts are clear rather than later when the key ideas become fuzzy."

Please recognize that more than 70 percent of the people that don't buy do so because they don't understand what you are selling, saying or trying to get them to believe. "Mr. Prospect, I'm glad you want to take time to think this over. How much time do you think you will need?" Get him to tell you days, minutes, months, weeks, whatever. "During that period of time what will you think about?" (Let him answer) What you're looking for is for him to verbalize what's in the back of his mind.

Don't try to get a prospect to change his mind once he had made up his mind. It is almost impossible to get him to change. The key is to get him to make a new decision based on new information. For example, "I really don't like that particular feature of your product." "Do you like the other features? Have you considered how the other feature of our product will help you satisfy your need, solve your problem, etc.?" Show him a new angle or viewpoint that he hadn't considered to enable him to make a new decision on the new information. Don't keep beating your head against the wall.

You and I are paid to answer sales questions. If a prospect could just pick up the telephone and call your company and say, "Send me one," salespeople would be unnecessary. Salespeople are there to solve problems, answer questions and facilitate the buying process. You are the most important part of the success of the free marketplace and sales questions are one of the most important aspects of the sales process.

Summary

Sales objections are not negative, but positive and necessary parts of a successful sale. Objections are really questions. They are a request for more information, a buying signal or a stall. They provide you with feedback that is important if you are to know and respond to the thinking of the prospect. Objections should not be defended, avoided or cause fear in your mind. Learn to encourage objections. Disarm them before they ever come up—or smoke them out of the subconscious mind of the prospect. If the same objections continually come up with different prospects, then you should restructure your sales presentation accordingly. Build your answer into your remarks. Learn to listen to the entire objection or question. Your prospects are telling you what you need to tell them to sell them.

Chapter Problem

You have a superior quality product in your market—but you are also the higher price supplier. How would you approach this?

_____

_____

_____

_____

_____

_____

_____

_____

_____

_____

_____

_____

Common Mistakes to Avoid

1. Treating the objection as an objection rather than a question.
2. Not practicing.
3. Lack of flexibility in answering objections.

Questions

1. What are sales objections (a definition, not examples)?
2. When should most objections be answered?
3. Should you always answer every objection?
4. What objection, more than any other, prevents a successful sale for you?
5. Why?
6. Why does a prospect stall?
7. Should you use canned or memorized answers to objections?
8. Would you like more objections? Why or why not?
9. What objections do you fear more than any other?

I've always made a total effort, even when the odds seemed entirely against me. I never quit trying; I never felt that I didn't have a chance to win.
—Arnold Palmer

Exercises

1. Develop your own answer to your most common objections and memorize and use them.
2. Redesign your presentation, bringing up your negative objections.
3. Change your attitude toward objections.

Visualization Exercises

Practice seeing yourself effectively handling all the objections you receive. Feel your prospect accepting your reasoning and answer.

Chapter Affirmations

I can effectively handle all the objections or questions my prospects have. Their objections only mean they are interested in my product or service.

I need objections to sell.

I will no longer fear but encourage objections. They are a sign of interest.

I take each meet one at a time.

—Jim Ryun

CLOSING THE SALE

Chapter Objectives

1. Closing is an art and a will to win.

2. Develop a closing strategy.

3. Learn to trial close.

4. Learn to close early and often.

No gains without pains.

—Ben Franklin

You can have a positive attitude and a well-qualified prospect; you can give an excellent presentation, successfully answer all the prospect's sales questions and represent a fine company with a quality product and outstanding reputation. If you don't get the order, however, you are a professional visitor. Ultimately, you get paid to close the sale.

The income you earn on the sale you almost make in your industry is, I'm sure, the same as in mine.

Many sales trainers and authors put the greatest emphasis on closing the sale. Entire courses, cassette programs and books have been created on "The Close of the Sale." What type of closer are you?

This is a basic question asked by all salespeople, whether they are selling an intangible service or tangible product. There are various shadings of all salespeople regarding their attitude toward their style of selling. These varied approaches can either heighten or reduce their selling effectiveness.

Let's discuss five different selling styles which can answer this question.

1. The Huckster: This is the type of salesperson whose only job is to get his product into his customer's hands, no matter whether or not it is needed or wanted. His orientation toward selling is to move his product using high pressure tactics.

2. The Personality Kid: This salesperson gets his job done by selling himself only. He charms his prospects into buying.

3. The Order Taker: This style of selling is very passive. His prospect needs the product or service and buys it. There is a lack of any interaction between buyer and seller.

4. Average Salesperson: This style of selling may be viewed as a mixture of selling both yourself and your product This salesperson presents both himself and his product by using standard selling techniques combined with showmanship. This is not marked by any true leadership or personal charisma.

5. The Professional Salesperson: This type of salesperson expands the view of his chosen profession by demonstrating to his prospects that he is selling a solution to a specific problem. This person's approach to the problem is to satisfy the prospect's wants and desires. He shows him how he will benefit by facing up to the problem and taking action. This person could be considered a problem- or want-creator and solver.

Which Are You?

The sales professional does common things in an uncommon way. I believe the close of the sales process is an important step, but by no means the most important step.

When you can do the common things in life in a uncommon way, you will command the attention of the world.
—George Washington Carver

Closing Is an Attitude

When do you begin to close a successful sale—at the end? In the middle? In the beginning? When do you sense that now is that right moment to go for the close? Do you close the prospect or let him close himself? Do you really need a seventh sense? These are all valid questions.

Experience tells me that there is not just one right time to close a sale. There are many times when a prospect is ready to buy. You must be able to control and be sensitive to these times. You cannot turn the responsibility for the close of a sale over to the prospect.

What is closing? Closing is not some mysterious thing, period, or word. It is not something that is tacked on to the end of your sales presentation. Closing is an attitude. It is a will to win! It is a desire to be of service. The close of a sale creates a win-win situation for the prospect and the salesperson. If only one of you wins, you both lose.

Many times salespeople think that they are poor closers. They are trying to turn a suspect into a customer at the close of a sale. This is virtually impossible. On the other hand, a well-qualified prospect from the beginning of the sales process will close himself or at least help you close the the sale sooner and easier. Your attitude should reflect that you are there to make a sale—not visit, educate, or make a friend. All of these are possible, only one pays the rent.

You and I both know there are many salespeople who don't belong in our profession, just as there are many teachers, nurses, lawyers, etc., that don't belong in their respective professions either. You can't change the world, but you can change yourself. Closing is understanding. Understanding yourself, understanding the prospect's fears, doubts, and wants—and understanding the psychology of closing.

Your success and happiness lie in you. Resolve to keep happy, and your joy and you shall form an invincible host against difficulties.
—Helen Keller

Closing Is an Art

Selling is an art form. Have you ever witnessed a professional salesperson closing a sale—not a closer closing a sale but a pro? Watch the skilled use of emotion, psychology, body language. You can feel the confidence and competence. You will also notice a gentle persuasion, a constant pressure, a compassion, and a spirit of cooperation. Let's call it emotional, psychological manipulation that is in the best interest of the prospect. To me, it is like watching a surgeon. The professional knows words, emotions, and feelings like the surgeon knows the body, his instruments, and his staff. But they didn't become that way overnight. The surgeon studies medicine. The professional salesperson studies people and human nature.

To successfully close a sale requires a sensitivity that comes with experience, practice and training. I believe this is why so many salespeople fear the close. They lack these ingredients.

Closing Sales or Closing Relationships?

Poor salespeople focus on just closing the sale. Successful salespeople focus on closing the sale and the relationship. Which is your approach?

For many salespeople, the close of the sale typically comes at the end of the sales presentation. It represents for many the final act in the sales process. It is unfortunate that these poorly informed and/or trained salespeople lack adequate understanding of the role of selling in today's competitive world.

Selling is not only about closing the current prospect on a particular product or service that solves one of their pressing problems, needs or desires. It is about building a trusting relationship and partnership with them by becoming a resource and helping them solve their ongoing problems or satisfy their continuing and evolving needs and desires.

Salespeople for years have been taught that to close a sale, they need to use devices or "closing techniques." For example, "the which would you prefer" or "get it before the price goes up" closes. These techniques, although sometimes successful, tend to focus only on how the current product or service solves a prospect's problem or satisfies a current need or want. The sales relationship must begin somewhere. The question is, how can you become a resource for a prospect, therefore beginning the relationship or partnership, before you have sold or closed this sale?

You must first evaluate your selling intent or philosophy that underlies the sales process and how it impacts your ability to close this sale and extend the future relationship.

If your focus is on the short-term versus the long-term, your intent is most likely only on moving products or services now. If your intent is to develop a long-term, mutually beneficial relationship with this new prospect, you may not sell this order, but that does not prevent you from beginning to build a positive relationship that can one day end in success.

It also depends on how you choose to define a successful sales relationship. All relationships, sales or otherwise, are dynamic. They are either getting better or getting worse. In order for a relationship to be getting better, there are several areas that need constant attention. They are: trust, respect, acceptance, integrity, communication, intent, the relationship direction, personal agendas, and a willingness to make the relationship work.

It is possible to begin to develop all of these with a prospect that you have not sold or "closed" yet. You can provide information, guidance, recommendations, solutions, feedback, and a variety of other services that would move the relationship from its current non-relationship status to one that is getting better.

I am not suggesting that you give away what you sell. If you sell information or guidance for example, don't give it away. That only weakens your ability to build a positive and successful win/win future relationship. But, if you sell widgets for example, is there some other area that you can help this prospect that strengthens you position in their eyes.

Let me give you an example. During the past twenty plus years as a speaker and trainer, I have given away hundreds of books and audio tapes by other speakers and authors to clients and prospects. You might wonder why I would introduce a competitor to a client. Do I have brain damage?

This philosophy has served me well for years for a number of reasons. One, it shows the prospect or client I am just as interested in their success as my own. Two, it communicates that I am secure enough in my own business that I am not threatened by other potential resources that are available to them. Three, it shows them I am on the lookout for information or ideas, that may or may not be related to what I do, that can contribute to their long-term success.

There have been many instances where I have sent these material to prospects and have not as yet done any business with them. But there are many more instances where this approach has helped me distance myself from my competitors. Customers want value today. By showing an interest in them before closing the sale, I am creating an impression. "If Tim does this much before he has sold us, we can assume he will do as much or more after we buy from him." Granted, once I sell them, I have set up a high expectation for service and results, so I better work as hard to keep and develop the business, but I will also lose the potential of using them to get referral business or the right to use them as a reference.

It takes more time, resources and energy to generate a new customer than it does to keep an existing one. It is also easier to do more business with a present customer that it is to find new ones. What is your approach? Are you investing a greater proportion of your time and resources to continue to find new business or to satisfy, develop and keep lifeblood of growth and success in sales; however, don't underestimate the ability to use your present customers to help you with that mission.

Next, few customers will just give you their business. You must ask for it, but you also have to earn the right to get it.

In my opinion, closing is more of a philosophy than a skill. It is more an attitude that a strategy. It is more about giving than getting, and it is more about service than your sales compensation.

What Is a Closing Philosophy or Attitude?

A closing attitude of philosophy says, "I am here to help you. I am here to do business with you. I am not on an educational crusade, nor am I a professional visitor." We all make the same income, regardless of what we sell, on the sales we don't close—nothing. But, successful salespeople leverage their time, energy, and resources by earning their customers' willingness to either directly sell new business for them or indirectly support their overall sales efforts with other potential customers.

Closing the sale or relationship is not something that begins at some magical point during the sales process; it is the attitude you bring to every good prospect selling situation. Notice I said good prospect. You will never turn a poor prospect into a customer with a quality product, an effective and persuasive sales message, or a tricky close, however, a well-qualified prospect will help you sell them. Keep in mind most people like to buy, but few people like to feel they are being sold to.

The Most Successful Closers Are Effective Prospectors

I recently read a survey of sales managers, the results of which were published in a national magazine. One of the questions was where they felt salespeople needed more regular quarterly training. The results of the participants to this question were as follows: 47 percent needed more training in consultative selling, 19 percent more training in closing, and only 5 percent in prospecting. That's like wanting your surgeon to focus 66 percent on their ability to conduct surgery and devote only 5 percent to getting information from a patient history, evaluation, tests, and so on. I don't know about you, but I am just as interested in an accurate evaluation or assessment of my condition as I am in their ability to relate to me, interpret the data, and then operate successfully. Their ultimate success will depend on the accuracy and timeliness of their earlier findings and their ability to uncover the real cause or issues.

These Managers Just Don't Get It

Prospecting is the most important sales skill when it relates to sales success. In the time you have spent reading this book, there have probably been at least a million salespeople try to close a sale somewhere. The ones that will have success will be those who were giving presentations to well-qualified prospects. The others are living in fantasy land and are not fooling anyone. They are only "logging" as many sales calls in a day or a week as they can to either satisfy the demands of management for adequate sales activity or to satisfy some misguided personal approach that will end with frustration, discouragement and failure.

When and How Often to Close

How early in the sales process should you close the sale? You may have heard the saying, "how many salespeople sell their product and then buy it back." They over-sell, over-educate and over-talk. Somehow it never seemed fair to me to make the prospect listen to your entire presentation, just because he was your only appointment that day. Sell the prospect, close the sale, then educate your customer. If they are ready to buy when you walk into their home or office—close the sale! Then tell them, "by the way, Mr. Prospect, there are a few important details that you should have."

The mind of a prospect must go through four stages psychologically. You must first get attention, then create interest, cause desire, and get action. If your presentation lasts thirty minutes, but the prospect is in step four when you arrive, there is no need to go through steps one through three.

It would amaze you how many salespeople talk their prospects out of buying without ever knowing it.

Closing as a Concept

Most people do not like to make decisions. They want things to happen, results to be gained, accomplishments to be made, and products to be bought, but they would prefer someone else relieve them of the pain of having to actually make the decision or choice.

When you are closing the sale, you must get a decision from the prospect, right? Wrong! We'll come back to this idea in a minute. Think back when you were giving your last sales presentation. You are about to pop the question—you are ready to ask for the order or for advance payment or a deposit. What happens to you? Physically? Emotionally? Psychologically? Have you ever been anxious, afraid, excited, nervous? Do your palms ever sweat? Did you ever swallow hard, notice your eyes leave the prospect, feel the tension in your face and body or your heart pound faster? If you are human, you experience some or all of these feelings from time to time.

By the way, what do you think your prospect is feeling at the close? Is he aware that you are going to ask for the order soon, or has he been sleeping? If your prospect is nervous, what do you think your nervousness is doing to his nervousness? Yes, it is intensifying it. What do you think your fear is doing to his fear, your excitement to his excitement? Intensifying it.

Any feelings that you have at the close of a sale, or for that matter, anytime during the sales process, you are transmitting to your prospect. It is therefore crucial that you control your own feelings during the sales process, but especially at the close.

These two ingredients, the prospect's desire to avoid a decision and this transference of feelings, can create what I like to call a psychological disaster. If it happens at the close, it can destroy the sale. If it occurs elsewhere you can still salvage the sale.

To remedy this problem, I suggest two things. First, move the entire sequence of the close to the beginning of the sales process as we discussed in Chapter Four under advance commitment.

Second, stop asking the prospect to make the buying decision. Who do you believe is in the best position to make the best decision for the prospect? The prospect or the salesperson? If you chose the prospect, you are wrong. Who is in the best position to make the best decision for the patient—the patient or the doctor?

You see, you know, or should know, his problems, and you should also know your own product line well enough to be in a positive position to make a good recommendation. Many times, the prospect doesn't know what he wants or what is best for him or how you can solve his problem, even after you've completed your presentation. A prospect for a home tells the realtor that he wants a three-bedroom, three-bath ranch in a rural area and ends up buying a four-bedroom Cape Cod in a populated development. Prospects are sometimes fickle and sometimes they are less than honest.

Let's take the buying decision away from the prospect. However, a decision must be made. You, the salesperson, should make the buying decision for the prospect. But how? For example, your typical close might go like this. "Well, that's the program, Mr. Prospect. Would you like to start on the first or the fifteenth of the month?" Here you are asking him to choose to make the buying decision. Let's just put a little twist in this method.

"Mr. Prospect, let's arrange for you to start on the first of the month, is that OK?" How is this method different from the first one? The minor change was by assuming he would start on the first and then stating it that way—"Let's arrange for you to start on the first." Then follow it with a statement that only asks him to agree with the decision you have made for him. He can either agree with your decision, or disagree with your choice. ("I can't start on the first.") If he does the latter, assume he will start on the fifteenth. Don't ask him at that point "Does that mean, Mr. Prospect, that you want to start on the fifteenth?" (Again, you are asking him to make a decision to start on the fifteenth.) Say, "Then, I'll set it up for the fifteenth." Once again, he'll either agree or he'll respond with a sales question.

The key to this method is two-fold. First, you have relieved the prospect of the buying decision. Prospects will agree with your decision all day long, but many of them, if asked, would not have made that same buying decision. This is a small psychological point, but believe me, this one idea can significantly increase your closing ratio. Second, he has three choices, two of which are in your favor. So, just by using this method, you have a 66 $2/3$ percent chance to close the sale. Try it, it works.

A Closing Plan

What do I mean by a closing plan? When you begin each sales presentation, do you have a thought-out sequence of statements or events that you follow as a guide to a more effective close? Are there certain signals that you look for, buying signals that trigger the beginning of the actual closing series?

Buying signals are key phrases, body language or questions that give you clues that the prospects may be ready to buy now. He might say something like, "Can I get thirty-day delivery, does that model come in blue, do you accept monthly payments, is this type of accident covered, is that adjacent lot available with the home?" All of these and hundreds of other questions could be buying clues. The prospect is in reality saying, "I want to buy, I'm trying to tell you, please make purchasing as painless for me as you can, help me make a decision."

Many salespeople are oblivious to most buying signals and literally thousands of potential sales are lost because of this. Listen carefully to what your prospects are trying to tell you and learn to react accordingly.

Trial Closing

When the prospect gives you a closing or buying clue or signal this is an excellent time to attempt a trial close. A trial close is any attempt to close the sale before you are officially finished with your complete presentation. When should you begin to trial close? As early in the sales process as you can. How often should you trial close? As often as you can. Most prospects are ready to buy before you think they are. By using trial closing type questions, you enable both you and the prospect to save time.

Here are a few sample trial closes that you might want to sprinkle throughout your presentation. "Mr. Prospect, have you got yourself convinced yet that this is a good program/product for you to take advantage of, or should I tell you more?" Either way, you can handle this. "How does this sound to you so far?" "What do you think of that benefit?" "Would that be important enough for you to get started today or should I continue with my demonstration?" Use your imagination. I'm sure you can come up with dozens of additional examples.

Buyer Fears

1. "Will I make a mistake if I buy?" Your prospect is concerned that he is doing the right thing. He needs constant reassurance as to the timeliness, intelligence, and general good sense of what he is doing.
2. "Will I get my money's worth?" "Will the product do what I am paying for it to do, or will this be another broken promise, lemon, or bad experience?" Again—reassurance.
3. "What will other people think of the decision I have made or about the product I am about to buy?" People like to brag about their good buys and decisions—it makes them look good. That's why we have housewarmings and when we buy a new car, we show it off to all our friends and relatives. On the other hand, a poor deal—a lemon—makes people look bad. So they are concerned about what their neighbors, parents, friends, associates, and others will think.

Customer Closing Fears

1. **Emotional block**—This is the fear that at any moment we are approaching the time for decision. People resist change and new things if they lack understanding or belief. Reassure the prospect with an appeal to his dominant emotional buying motive.

2. **Cultural block**—This is the tendency to maintain the status quo—not to change. "We've never lived in a two-story, never had car trouble, always advertised only in the newspaper, done our own training." Change for these people goes against all they have been taught or conditioned to believe. To deal with this fear, you should appeal to the prospect from the practical or economical standpoint. Show him how change, a new approach, program or service will save him money, time, and convenience over the way things have always been done.

3. **Perceptual block**—A perceptual block is the temporary skepticism of a new idea. The best way to handle this fear is to show the prospect how other products that were at one time new and uncommon are now well-accepted. For example, there was a time when town houses were not well-received. Are they now in your market? Can you think of any other examples?

A Closing Sequence

The average attention span of most adults is eight seconds. Most people think about 50,000 thoughts a day, or about one thought every three seconds or twenty a minute. Let's say your presentation lasts thirty minutes. How much of what you have covered do you think your prospect heard or remembers? Don't flatter yourself. Very little!

I suggest that just prior to closing the sale or quoting a price, you review the highlights of your presentation. This review should take at most two or three minutes. Its purpose is to focus your prospect's attention in a short period of time on the positive points or benefits of your product. Obviously, I would not review the negatives. "Mr. Prospect, we have covered a lot of ground here today. Let's take a minute or two and review what we have discussed. You may recall...You indicated that you particularly...We discussed...You were excited about...We said we…and so on." What you are doing, in a concentrated period of time, is building value in the prospect's mind so that when you give him the price, it will seem small by comparison. Don't just rely on your presentation. Review all the positive highlights.

Method of Closing

Alternatives of Choice: Always ask for an answer to a choice of two, never only one. For example: Wrong—"Do you want to give me a deposit today?" Right—"Would you prefer to give me cash or a check as a deposit?" Here, you are assuming he is going to give you a deposit. Your choice to him is what form it will take. Wrong—"Should I arrange for settlement on the fifteenth of the month?" Right—"Would the first or the fifteenth of the month be better for settlement for you?"

Sharp Angle: This is an effective close to use with a buying signal.
Question: "Can I start on the fifteenth of the month?"
Answer: "Do you want to start on the fifteenth of the month?" When you answer his question with just a simple "yes," all you have is an answered question. The second way, if he answers "yes," he's closed the sale.
Question: "Can I pay in monthly installments?" The concept here is simple. Just keep in mind the idea, "Do you want it if I can? Do you want to if it does? Will you if I can arrange it?"
Answer: "Do you want to pay in monthly installments?"

Order Blank: This is probably the simplest and oldest close in the book: All you do is ask a question, the answer to which is some piece of information that you put on your application, agreement, invoice, or order form. "Mr. Prospect, what is the correct billing address?" The key here is not to say anything—let the prospect answer—or object. Either way, you can handle the situation. "Mr. Prospect, what is your middle initial?" When he answers, put the information on your order form and immediately go on to another question.

Storytelling: In the storytelling close you tell a story about a customer that had a problem, need or want similar to that of your current prospect. At the close of the story, you tell your prospect how the customer made a favorable decision and had a positive outcome as a result. Your prospect psychologically will substitute himself in your story, thereby seeing himself making a favorable decision and having a positive outcome.

Many salespeople feel storytelling is a corny approach. Believe me, it will work if the story is true and you use a little showmanship when telling it. Remember, you need to be a little bit of a ham to succeed in this business.

Puppy Dog: Let them have it for a while and it will soon be theirs. We're selling typewriters, copy machines, trial memberships, etc., that way. Some products, obviously, don't lend themselves to this technique directly, but they do indirectly. For example, you can't let the prospect live in the new home for a month and then have him decide that he doesn't like it. But, what you can do in this instance is create the event in mind pictures. "Mr. Prospect, imagine how this room would look with your furniture here." "Mr. Prospect, imagine attending your next business meeting carrying this fine briefcase."

Secondary Question: In this method you follow-up your major closing question with a minor question. The concept here is that the prospect may hesitate to answer the major questions, but will happily answer the minor question. If the sentence is structured properly, the answer to the minor question will make it unnecessary to answer the major question. For example, "Mr. Prospect, would you prefer the ranch or the Cape, and would you like to use your settlement attorney or ours?" "Mr. Prospect, would you like to enroll for one year or two and would you like to use your pen or mine?" "Mr. Prospect, would you prefer the term or whole life plan and would you like the policy to take effect on the first or the fifteenth of the month?"

The key here is to get a commitment to the sale on the minor point. Then work out the details of the major question with a customer, not a prospect.

Ben Franklin Balance Sheet: The Ben Franklin Balance Sheet works, but you have to use it and you need the credibility of old Ben. It goes like this—"Mr. Prospect, we have a very revered man in our American history. His name is Ben Franklin. Many times Ben would find himself in a position similar to that which you find yourself today. If it was the right thing to do, Ben wanted to do it and it it was the wrong thing, he wanted to be sure and avoid it. Isn't that about the way you feel today? If it's the right thing to do, you want to be sure and do it. If it's the wrong thing to do you want to be sure and avoid it." Let him answer.

"Let's do what Ben did on these occasions. (See Figure 6-A) Ben would take out a plain sheet of paper and draw a line down the middle. Would you do that please? He would then write at the top of the left side—Reasons For—and on the top of the right side—Reasons Against; would you write that also? Let's think of as many reasons as we can favoring your decision today." Then he comes up with one. You add four. He adds one. You add three. He adds two. You add five. Where are you getting all these items to add to the plus side? From your list of features that you made in Chapter Four, Figure 4-C. (See page 155)

> *Only a mediocre is always at his best.*
> —M. Somerset Maugham

"Now, let's think of how many reasons there are against your decision today." And then, you shut up. You don't help. Rarely will the prospect ever come up with more than three or four "nos" compared to 25–30 reasons for a sale—his mind can't switch fast enough from the yes to the no side to be effective. "I guess it's fairly obvious what your decision should be. What is your middle initial?" When you use the Ben Franklin Balance Sheet you must follow this close with a second close immediately.

The Final Step

Once the sale has been closed, this is the time to ask for referrals. Don't wait or put it off to later in the sales process. This is the moment that the prospect is the most sold on you and your product. Take advantage of the psychology. I close every sale with a thank you for your business, congratulations, you have made a wise decision and a reassuring statement, something like, "You will be very pleased with our product, program, service." Just mention some general positive benefits the prospect. will gain. This moment is an emotional high for the salesperson and an emotional low or moment of defeat for the prospect. Leave behind a positive, enthusiastic, confident, self-assured customer. Otherwise, you may get a phone call or letter of cancellation.

The worst sin toward our fellow creatures is not to hate them, but to be indifferent to them; that's the essence of humanity.
—George Bernard Shaw

Chapter Summary

Closing is a will to win—an art. It is not a series of cute phrases designed to outwit or outmaneuver the prospect. People generally do not like to make decisions. Closing is not getting your prospect to make a buying decision, but getting him to agree with the buying decision you have made for him. The close of a sale is the natural conclusion to a well-executed sales presentation. Closing is not something you suddenly begin at the end of the sales process. You start to close at the beginning. You are there to sell—not to visit. The commissions you earn on the sales you almost make are the same in all industries. You must close the sale or you are just a professional conversationalist. The responsibility for the close, however, is yours, not the prospect's. You are, or should be, in the best position to make the best decision for him.

Figure 6-A

BEN FRANKLIN BALANCE SHEET

Reasons for:	Reasons against:

Chapter Problem

The prospect is interested—you've completed your presentation. He says he'll take the information to his board of directors for a decision tomorrow morning! What would you do?

_____

_____

_____

_____

_____

_____

_____

_____

_____

_____

_____

_____

_____

Common Mistakes to Avoid

1. Quitting after only one "no."
2. Attempting to close before value has been established.
3. Selling price instead of quality.

Chapter Questions

1. What is closing?
2. When do you start to close?
3. How many times should you attempt to close?
4. Name several methods of closing.
5. Write out your closing sequence, word for word.
6. What are the characteristics of a closing attitude?
7. What is your closing ratio? Is it improving?
8. What is an objection at the close?
9. What words should be used during the close?
10. What words should be avoided during the close?

Great talkers, little doers.

—Ben Franklin

Exercises

1. Memorize a new close each week and practice it daily.
2. Develop a list of trial closes.

Visualization Exercise

It's almost time to pop the key closing question. See yourself relaxed, confident and calm. But also see yourself in control. Your prospect is ready to buy, but he is waiting for your cue. He wants to buy—now close the sale.

Chapter Affirmations

My prospects want to buy from me. They are ready to buy now. My prospects have the ability and desire to make a favorable buying decision today. I am a strong, confident closer. I will close this sale now. If my prospect does not buy today, it is not because of me, but his lack of desire at the time.

Win or lose, playing at all is winning.

—Wolfgang Nording

MAINTAINING SALES RECORDS

SELLING RULE: NUMBER 7

Sales records are an absolute must—keep them—analyze them—learn from them.

Chapter Objectives

1. How to develop the right attitude toward sales records.

2. How to keep records.

3. How to analyze the records for growth.

4. How to get out of a sales slump.

7

Diligence is the mother of good luck.
—Ben Franklin

Why did I want to win? Because I didn't want to lose.
—Max Schmelling

Introduction

Most people that are failing in sales do not know why, whereas most of the highly successful salespeople can tell you in an instant what they do exceptionally well and where they are the strongest. This knowledge comes from good sales records. In my experience, I have found most salespeople do not like to keep records and most do not keep adequate records other than those their company requires.

Do you keep sales records regularly or only when you are beginning to feel yourself sliding? Records will not make you successful but they can be of great help in guiding you in the right direction.

The first thing to do in life is to do with purpose what one proposes to do.
—Pablo Casals

Why Keep Records?

If you can quickly answer the following questions, I'll bet you are consistently keeping, analyzing, and learning from your records. If you cannot, I urge you to carefully read this chapter and implement its suggestions.

1. What is your average sales volume?
2. What is your average commission per sale?
3. What is your average number of sales per month? Week? Day?
4. How many closing presentations do you give per week?
5. How is your average number of new prospects generated in a week?
6. What percentage of your business comes from referrals? Advertising? Cold calling, etc.?
7. How many new prospects do you need per week to keep your qualified prospect pipeline full?
8. What is your closing ratio? What is the ratio of your number of sales to complete presentations?
9. What is your interview termination percentage?
10. What is your average sales presentation worth in both volume and commission? What is each contact worth? Each telephone call? Each new referral? Each appointment? (To determine these ratios, divide the number of telephone calls by your total monthly sales or income and repeat the process for each example.)
11. How many telephone calls must you make to get one appointment? One closing presentation? One sale?
12. What is your ratio of new prospects to sales?
13. What percentage of your business is from existing customers? New customers?
14. What is your per customer renewal rate? Upgrade rate? Cancellation rate?
15. How many referrals do you get from your average customer?

After completing these fifteen questions, you are probably either encouraged by what you learned or disgusted.

Well-kept records can steer you in the right direction and help you avoid the dead ends, frustrations, and anxiety of sales slumps.

A sales slump is when you are temporarily motivated by method rather than results. One of the best ways to avoid a sales slump is with a daily, weekly or monthly goal program. To improve your selling results, you should set activity goals rather than productivity goals.

If salespeople consistently have the right type of selling activity, eventually they will have the results that they both expect and deserve.

When you set activity goals it is much easier to track both activity and productivity results.

You can also more effectively determine weaknesses and areas where improvement can take place. Many times this will give you the motivation to go on.

There is in most of us a tendency to relax after a successful day, sale or month. Let's face it, you deserve a break. You stop for a moment to bask in your well-deserved success. However, this fleeting moment can become a longer period of time which ultimately slows your momentum.

One way to avoid these highs and lows is to graph your activity and results day by day, week by week, month by month, and if you choose, year by year.

Comparing your relative successes and failures in this way graphically demonstrates in an easy-to-picture method, the trend or direction of your ability in a certain area. For example: Let's say the month of January you averaged fifty telephone calls per week, twenty appointments per week and three sales with a total volume of $10,000 and an income of $1,000. Your income goal is $2,000 per month. You have several choices or directions.

1.   Increase your number of presentations by 100 percent. (This could only come from better telephoning, by increasing your ratio from 20/50 to 40/50).

2.   Improving your closing skills to improve your closing ratio from 3/20 to 6/20.

3.   Improving your prospecting so that you only give your presentations to better qualified prospects—ten presentations/three sales or twenty presentations/six sales.

4.   Selling more per customer by increasing the average size of your order. Instead of three sales $10,000, we have one or two sales $20,000.

Figure 7-A gives you an example of how your monthly chart might look.

The secret of success is this: there is no secret of success.

—Elbert Hubbard

Figure 7-A

	Line	Jan.	Feb.	March	April	May
Telephone calls	1	100	75	50	40	50
Appointments	2	60	60	40	20	10
Sales	3	10	20	20	10	8
Average volume/sale	4	$1,000	$2,000	$2,000	$3,000	$2.000
Average income/sale	5	$100	$200	$200	$300	$200
Closing ratio	6	1/6	1/3	1/2	1/2	4/5
Ratio telephone/ appointment	7	6/10	6/7	4/5	1/2	1/5
Total volume	8	$10,000	$20,000	$20,000	$30,000	$16,000
Total income 10% commission	9	$1,000	$2,000	$2,000	$3,000	$1,600

Let's carefully analyze these numbers and ratios from this sample chart, what they mean and how they can help you.

1. Why did our number of telephone calls decrease per month from January through May? Time off? Call reluctance? Fewer prospects to call? Poor time management?

2. Why did our telephone to appointment percentage stay the same between January and February? Better telephone techniques? Better prospects?

3. Why did our telephone call to appointments drop to only one in five in May? Poor telephone closing? Poor prospects?

4. Why did our sales increase by 100 percent from January to February with the same number of appointments? Better prospects? Improved sales presentation? Better closing techniques?

5. Why did our average volume per sale increase with fewer appointments in April? Why did it decrease in May?

6. Why did our closing ratio improve between January and May?

Figure 7-B

Monthly Record

Month _____

Telephone calls: Personal calls: Overall totals:

	1	2	3	4	5	6	7	8	9	10	11	12	13	14	15	16	17	18	19	20	21	22	23
Date	Total	Apt. pres.	Apt. made	Sales pres.	Sales	Vol.	Serv.	Ref.	C.C.	Apts	Serv	Pres.	Close	Sales	Vol.	Ref.	Sales	Vol.	Ref.	Comm.	Avg. sale	Avg. comm

1ST WEEK TOTAL

2ND WEEK TOTAL

3RD WEEK TOTAL

4TH WEEK TOTAL

Monthly Total _____ Last month's total _____ Same month last year total _____ Best Month Ever Total _____ Worst Month Ever Total _____

KEY

1. Date–Action Taken
2. Total Telephone Calls Attempted
3. Appointment Telephone Presentations Made
4. Appointments Made
5. Actual Telephone Sales Presentations Made
6. Number Sales Made

7. Total Sales Volume
8. Service Telephone Calls Made
9. Referrals obtained
10. Cold-Calls Made
11. Appointments Kept
12. Service Appointments

13. Presentation Given
14. Interviews Where You Attempted To Close
15. Sales Made
16. Total Volume
17. Referrals obtained

18. Total Sales Made
19. Total Sales Volume
20. Total Referrals
21. Total Commissions Earned
22. Average Sale
23. Average Commission Per Sale

7. If you wanted to increase your income, where would improve-
    ment be most rewarding? Per sale volume? Closing ratio? Ratio
    of telephone calls to appointments? Fewer appointments but
    better prospects?
8. Do you notice any potential trouble spots to be aware of?
9. Any significant danger signals?
10. Where did you improve the most during this period? All of this
    information can enhance your selling ability, use of time, self-
    improvement, income, personal satisfaction, and self-esteem. It is
    important to know where you're good and that you are consis-
    tently improving. We all need to know we are growing positively.

The reason why worry kills more people than work is that more people
worry than work.

—Robert Frost

Records and You

You may now suspect that there is more to effective record keeping than you
have ever imagined. Don't be misled. You are creating records, good or bad,
whether you keep them or not—or whether you accept them or not.

It is not really difficult to keep good sales records. The key is to form
the daily habit. Make it a regular part of your normal sales activity.

One method would be to use a 3" x 5" card and record daily all your
selling activity. Then spend two or three minutes at the end of your day
transferring the information to a master monthly sheet. (See Figure 7-B)
Once you have begun to analyze your selling results, ratios and activity
weaknesses, you can begin to set daily goals to improve your activity. For
example, refer back to Figure 7-C. In May you notice a drastic dropoff in
appointments. A June goal could then be twenty appointments for the
month or five per week or one per day.

Be careful of selling goals too far out and not breaking them down
into smaller steps. For example, in Figure 7-C, a goal in June might be
to increase your telephone call to appointment ratio from one in five to
five in five. Why not set a shorter range goal equal to your previous best

month (four out of five). It is demotivating to continue to set long-term goals and always fall short. Learn to break your activity goals down to the smallest increment of time.

Record-keeping takes self-discipline, commitment and practice. But I guarantee you increased income if you will keep, refer to, and learn from your records.

Chapter Summary

Well-kept sales records can prevent sales slumps and improve sales results and efficiency. Records can contribute greatly to your ultimate success in professional selling. But, you must keep them, analyze them, and adjust your selling behavior as a result of what you learn from them.

Most salespeople who are failing cannot tell you why. On the other hand, most of the superstars can tell you exactly where they are strong and why they are effective. Most salespeople hate the task of record-keeping and the details that result. It's a matter of habit. Either you form the habit of keeping records or you do not.

Common Mistakes to Avoid

1. No consistency in record keeping.
2. Keeping but not evaluating records.
3. Dishonesty with yourself in your record keeping (you'll only hurt yourself).

Questions

1. How can sales records prevent a sales slump?
2. How can sales records improve your sales results and income?
3. Why don't you (if you don't) keep better records?
4. What are the most important ratios? Why?
5. What can you learn from your records?
6. Does your management require sales reports or records?
7. Are they sufficient to guide your successful career progress?

Exercises

1. Keep a complete diary of sales records for thirty days.
2. Compute all ratios as described in this chapter once a week.
3. Repeat this process for one more month and compare the two sets of ratios.

Win or lose, do it fairly.

—Knute Rockne

AFTER-SALES SERVICE

Chapter Objectives

1. Why give service.

2. How to service.

3. When to service.

4. Who to service.

8

In this world, men are saved not by faith, but by the want of it.
—Ben Franklin

He that sells upon trust loses many friends and always wants money.
—Ben Franklin

Introduction

When is service actually service? You might think that question is redundant. I don't think it is. Many people look at service as what their service department provides or sales support personnel provide.

In this chapter, we're not referring to this as service. My concept of after-sales service is what you do after the sale has been made and the product has been delivered. What type of contract do you have with your customer or client on a regular basis? Does your conscience ever send you messages like—"I wonder if my customer is still using the product; I wonder if he is still glad he bought. Has he done business with any other supplier since he became my client?"

Do you have the type of relationship with your client that he would not call you first before cancelling an order, reducing an order, asking for a price quote or bid from a competitor?

Or, do you have the type of client relationship where the client asks you for advice on matters not relating to your product or service, voluntarily calls a friend or business associate to sell you (without your asking), gives you carte blanche with his budget to solve his problems, or takes your suggestions without question or reservations?

Which type relationship do you have? Why not review your customers based on the past twelve months, and ask yourself, "How am I doing with each?" Customers can sometimes be fickle. Sometimes they demand a lot of care and attention and other times they really don't want to see you for months.

Do they want regular telephone contact? Personal visits? Written correspondence? Or, do they have a don't call us, we'll call you attitude?

You can just as easily destroy a good relationship with too much of the wrong kind of service as you can with too little of the right

When the sale has been closed, you might ask questions like: How often would you like your program reviewed? Under what conditions or circumstances would you like me to review your situation? I like to keep abreast of my client's needs and situations as they change. When would you suggest we get together again? Of the other salespeople that serve you, which service do you like best and why?

All of these questions, although they do not set specific parameters, can give you some clues as to the type of contact your new client would like.

Never look down to test the ground before taking your next step: only he who keeps his eye fixed on the far horizon will find his right road.
—Dag Hommarskjold

Potential Business

There is another method that you should use to determine the amount and type of service you give a client.

Let's assume you are now doing 20 percent of client A's business, and this 20 percent represents 10 percent of your total business. If you could double your business with this client, you could almost have 25 percent of your sales from one account.

Client B provides you with five percent of your business, but you also have 100 percent of his business.

One important factor to analyze is the potential business of a particular client and the real possibility of getting that business. I would give more individual attention to client A than B. Now, I didn't say ignore B, but give him only what he expects. I would go the extra mile with client A.

Going the Extra Mile

This is doing more than expected of you, doing more because you want to, and doing more not with the idea that you will be repaid—although you will be (but maybe not from that client).

Develop the attitude: I want to do more, not less, than is necessary for a particular customer.

Going the extra mile has always been my rule for living when it comes to service. Remember the story of Earl Nightingale's Stove of Life?

Now, stove, give me some heat, then I'll put some wood in. Make me the supervisor, then I'll do more work. Give me the raise, then I'll earn it.

It doesn't work that way! And you know it. First, you put the wood in. Then you get the heat out. First, you provide good service, then you earn the right to get more business.

I feel that the greatest reward for doing is the opportunity to do more.
—James E. Salk

Types of Service

Regular personal contact: Some customers just want to see your face regularly. They like you and that was one of the reasons they bought. Most people are hungry for personal strokes. "If I can get mine from a salesperson—because he is nice to me, respects me, or just listens to me once in a while, that's all right." Other customers won't mind seeing you often, but they dislike the approach—"I was in the neighborhood and thought I'd stop by to say hello." (That communicates I had nothing to do, assume you didn't either, so here I am). Rather than just stopping by for a visit, why not bring your customer an idea that can help him—something constructive: information on trends, new models, what other people in his same business are doing or thinking. If you're always full of good, positive ideas and are willing to share them, you will be amazed how much people will look forward to seeing you.

Written Contract. There are several forms of written contact that you can have with a customer:

1. A personal handwritten note.
2. A monthly formal written letter.
3. A regular newsletter of some type. You can write your own or you can purchase various newsletters and have your logo imprinted on them. These come in a number of subjects—taxes, finances, real estate, banking, insurance, and more.
4. Copies of reprints of articles from magazines, newspapers or newsletters that you know are of interest to your customers.
5. Copies of newsclips that either feature your client or someone you know he knows or would like to keep abreast of.
6. Thank you cards, birthday cards, anniversary cards, and major holiday cards.

Use your imagination. I'm sure you can come up with other ideas.

Telephone contact. I recommend you touch base with your best clients at least once a month by telephone. I would suggest you set up one afternoon a week just for service calls. You'll be amazed at what you will turn up in the way of problems, or opportunities. Have a different message each month. One month, an idea. Next, a request for a referral. Next, a general inquiry—how is the program, product, etc., working? Next, ask for a personal evaluation of yourself and so on. The calls don't have to be long, but form a habit of regular telephone contact with your best clients. It will pay big dividends.

If you achieve success, you will get applause, and if you get applause, you will hear it. My advice to you concerning applause is this: enjoy it but never quite believe it.

—Robert Montgomery

After-sale Follow-up

When should after-sale service begin? Before the sale has actually been closed. The close represents the beginning of a customer-salesperson relationship. That relationship cannot be transferred to some other person or department in your organization. You have a responsibility to that customer as long as he is using your product or service. If, for some reason, there is a problem with delivery, billing, your service department, it is your responsibility to immediately communicate the situation or status, and any appropriate action that you are taking, to the customer. Until the service has been rendered or the product has been delivered, you should maintain open lines of communication at all times with the customer. It is not his responsibility to make you aware of problems or shortcomings. It is yours to learn about them as they happen. My philosophy here is—the best surprise is no surprise for you or the client.

If there was nothing wrong in the world there wouldn't be anything for us to do.
—George Bernard Shaw

After-sale Problems

Sometimes things go wrong. People make mistakes and machines make mistakes. Your role as a salesperson is to act as an intermediary between the customer and the company. Your face and person may be the only human contact he will ever have. If things go wrong, the customer may blame you, rightly or wrongly. This is life. The customer paid his money and didn't get, for whatever reason, what he paid for. He wants it replaced, corrected, or credited.

In all situations it is your responsibility to correct the problem and leave a happy customer behind.

Sometimes in the pressures of the day you consider a good sale made, and psychologically you want to forget it and go on to new sales calls and new successes. But, many times an after-sale problem crops up at the worst possible time. If you will learn to not be surprised or shocked by problems, you will go a long way toward enjoying a peaceful sales career. The by-words for after-sales problems should be: remain calm, poised, flexible, open minded, friendly, tactful, and easy going. Blame, needless hurry, and anger only aggravate the situation. Evaluate the problem, consider alternatives, make a decision, and communicate with the client. Not facing the problem doesn't make it go away either physically or in the prospect's mind. In fact, he will have more respect for you if you have the courage to face a problem on his behalf and solve it without whining or complaining.

Solving an after-sale problem is actually an opportunity to prove to the customer that you meant what you said when you told him you would give him good service.

Getting Repeat Business through Service

The way to deserve more business from the same customer is to make him glad every day that he did business with you. Let your service sell for you. If you are not getting additional business from your current customers, maybe it is because they are unhappy with the product, the company or you. You better find out why and then correct the situation.

Conscience is the inner voice that warns us somebody may be looking.
—H.L. Mencken

Anything Offered for Sale Needs Selling to Be Sold

If you want more business from your current customers, it's easy. Once you deserve it (by providing good service), just ask. It's that simple. Many salespeople take the attitude of "take the money and run." They feel lucky to have the business they do and hesitate to ask for more. They don't want to rock the boat. If the business is there and you don't ask for it, your competitors will. You can't afford to wait. Your customer bought once. He will buy again. Look at it from his point of view. "I bought once. I'm sure that since my original purchase there must be new models, programs, etc., that have been developed. I wonder why my salesperson doesn't keep me up-to-date. Maybe it is because this product, service, etc., is no longer competitive. Maybe I should shop around next time." Your lack of service creates doubt in the mind of the prospect.

Getting Sales Support

This will be the shortest section in the book. To get sales support, use frequently the words "please" and "thank you for your help."

Chapter Summary

Do you think you give good after-sale service? If you can complete all of the following questions positively, you probably do. If not, you have some room for improvement.

Has your customer only bought from you since your relationship began?

Is your customer buying only from you now?

Have you re-evaluated your customer's needs on a regular basis since your first sale to him?

Do you contact your customers regularly?

Is your customer still happy with your product or service?

If his original buying conditions were to develop again, would you get the business? Are you sure?

Common Mistakes to Avoid

1. Dodging unhappy customers.
2. Shifting blame for your after-sales problems to the service department or management.
3. Thinking that service is when you return to sell more.

Promises may fit the friends, but non-performance will turn them into enemies.
—Ben Franklin

Questions

1. Define good after sale-service.
2. Why do customers buy from your competitors?
3. Is solving after-sale problems considered service?
4. When you increase or upgrade your customers' purchases from you, is that service?
5. How much service is too much?

6. Should you service all your customers the same way?
7. Have you ever lost a customer because of poor service?
8. What have you done so that it doesn't happen again?
9. Whose responsibility is service?
10. Are you ever justified in not giving service?

Exercises

1. Develop and implement a schedule of client follow-up contact.
2. Schedule and implement a written follow-up program.

Never look back, someone might be gaining on you.
—Satchel Page

INDEX

BOOK CLOSING

Dear Reader,

I hope you enjoyed reading *Soft Sell* as much as I enjoyed writing it. I hope you found this to be a valuable learning experience and that the application of its contents will pay you dividends of increased sales and income for years to come.

Thank you for sharing your life with me and taking the time to read this book.

Please remember always: School is never out for the Pro. My best wishes for your continued success, happiness, and prosperity.

—Tim Connor

ABOUT THE AUTHOR

 Tim Connor, CSP is the president of the Connor Resource Group Inc. He has been a full-time speaker, trainer, and consultant since 1974. He has given over 3,000 presentations worldwide on Sales, Management, Motivation, Customer Service, Managing Change, Team Building, and Building Positive Relationships.

He has also facilitated strategic planning retreats and executive management meetings for many of his clients and is a "results oriented" consultant and coach to many business owners, managers and executives.

Over 85 percent of his engagements have been repeat presentations for the same clients presenting fresh new ideas each time.

He is the author of four books including the international best seller, *Soft Sell,* now in its twentieth printing and a new inspirational classic. He is the author of *The Voyage, a Journey of Self-discovery,* and numerous custom audio and video learning systems as well as the popular newsletter, *Life Balance.*

Tim has been a member of the National Speakers Association since 1978, and received his CSP (certified speaking professional) designation from the NSA in 1990. Only 300 members of this international organization of 4,000 members have earned this exceptional designation since 1974.

Tim is more than a speaker, trainer, and consultant. He has been a valuable resource for each of his clients for over twenty years.

He lives in Davidson, N.C.

Tim Connor, CSP
Connor Resource Group, Inc.
20033 Davidson Concord Rd.
Davidson, NC 28036
(704) 895-1230 • (704) 895-1231 *fax*
(800) 222-9070 • (800) 222-9071 *fax*